Gregor Weichbrodt

Dictionary of non-notable Artists

Frohmann Verlag / 0x0a

Gregor Weichbrodt is part of the writers' collective 0x0a.
More info at www.ggor.de and www.0x0a.li

This is a Frohmann Verlag and 0x0a project, released on Sep 29, 2016.
http://frohmann.orbanism.com

© 2016 by Gregor Weichbrodt and Frohmann Verlag, Christiane Frohmann

Sources: Wikipedia, "Articles for deletion", 2006/12/16 – 2016/09/14.
Cover design and layout: Gregor Weichbrodt

ISBN Paperback: 978-3-3944-195-42-1

Die Deutsche Nationalbibliothek verzeichnet diese Publikation in der Deutschen Nationalbibliografie; detaillierte bibliografische Daten sind im Internet über http://dnb.d-nb.de abrufbar.

Contents

Actor

Amanda Aardsma
non-notable actress/former beauty queen.

Owen Aaronovitch
non-notable actor.

Aarushi
The actress is not famous.

Peter Abbay
Non-notable actor.

Dalton Abbott
Non-notable actor with only one credit to his name (at the age of two).

Chris Ackerman
Non-notable actor with only 1 major starring role.

Robert Ackerman
Non-notable actor.

Arthur Adams
Non-notable actor.

Jack Adams
Non-notable actor.

Faye Adell
Non-notable actress who had minor roles in mostly non-notable German films/TV shows.

Prachee Adhikari
Non-notable actress.

Nivas Adithan
Very minor actor who has only been active since early-mid 2012.

Swati Aggarwal
Non-notable actress.

Greg Akcelrod
Akcelrod is not an actor, he only played as an extra in two movies not released.

Mohamed Akhzam
Actor with just one role.

Joshua Alba
Non-notable actor.

Antonio Albadran
Non-notable actor.

Dion Albanese
Actor with one credit to his name, a bit part in a movie 40 years ago.

Aaron Albert
Actor with no major roles or significant recurring roles.

Alejandro Alcondez
Non-notable actor.

Enrique Alejandro
Non-notable actor.

Brandi Alexander
Bit-former Miss Universe Canada pageant contestant who came outside the top 10, part actress and eliminated contestant on Canada's Next Top Model.

Richard Alexander
Non-notable actor.

Steff Alexander
Non-notable actress, appears to have been in only one thing.

Elle Alexandra
Non-notable Pron actor lacking GHITS and GNEWS of substance.

Teddy alexandro-evans
Non-notable actor.

Rohan Ali
Non notable Bollywood actor and model.

Daniel Allar
Allar is non-notable actor who had very minor role in the series Prison Break and he appeared in only four episodes.

Michael Alldredge
Non-notable actor.

Tyrees Allen
Non-notable actor.

Chris M. Allport
Non-notable minor actor, apparently most notable for "dubb[ing] the crowing sounds for Robin Williams" in a scene in Hook.

Sana Althaf
Actress who falls under way too soon-only 2 roles so far.

Rachel Ambler
Non-notable actress.

Chace Ambrose
Non-notable actor, director and newscaster.

Utkarsh Ambudkar
Not a notable actor.

Aron Anazia
Non notable actor/producer/director.

Jerad Anderson
Non-notable actor and musician.

Amy Anderssen
Doesn't meet the notability requirements for pornographic actors.

Christopher Andrews
Non-notable actor and writer.

Zora Andrich
actress of questionable notability, seems to have had only a single passing bit of notability on a reality show

Chet Anekwe
Non-notable actor lacking Ghits and GNEWS of substance.

Jerry G. Angelo
Non-notable actor/producer.

Chriss Anglin
Non-notable actor.

Jeremy Applegate
Non-notable actor.

Ayelet Argaman
Non-notable actress.

Darryl Armbruster
Non-notable actor.

Adam Arnold
Non-notable child actor.

Avital Ash
Non-notable actor lacking GHits of substance and with no GNEWS.

Brad Ashten
Non-notable actor.

Jessica Ashworth
An actress.

Asif Imrose
Non-notable actor.

Nozomi Aso
There is no indication that Aso comes anywhere near meeting the notability requirements for pornogrpahic actresses.

William Atkinson
Non-notable actor with only minor, one-off roles that are often uncredited.

Paulo Avelino
Unnotable actor, a contestant on reality TV show StarStruck (Philippine TV series), only two credits, both bit parts.

Brian Avery
Non-notable actor.

Kristian Ayre
Unnotable actor.

James Babson
Non-notable actor.

Tom Babson
Doesn't seem to be notable, either as an ice hockey coach, or as an actor.

Dave Baez
Non-notable actor.

Ainsley Bailey
Not a notable actor.

Greg Baker
Non-notable actor.

Robert Baker
Non-notable actor.

Morgan Val Baker
Actor who has 2 issues-first only 2 roles and 2nd, notable for being a

grandson to someone famous.

Catherine Balavage
Non-notable actress

Julien Ball
Non-notable actor.

Mahnoor Baloch
Unnotable actress.

Bambadjan Bamba
Non-notable actor.

Helia Bandeh
Non-notable dancer and actress.

Russell Geoffrey Banks
Unknown actor, never had notable roles.

Quinn Bard
Non-notable actor.

Prakash Bare
Non-notable actor and producer.

Guy V. Barfield
Nonnotable actor.

Mookie Barker
Non-notable actor.

Kemi Baruwa
Non notable actor.

Joe Bays
Non-notable actor.

Ann Beach
Actress who appears to have a number of small roles, but little of importance.

Drew Beasley
Non-notable teenage actor.

Scott Beaudin
Non-notable actor.

Sterling Beaumon
A minor actor, both in age and in terms of actual impact.

Lorna Bennett
Actor who appears to have only had small parts in several TV shows and short films.

Stephen Beresford
Unotable actor with only a few credits that he has had.

Michelle Bernard
Non-notable minor actor lacking GHits and GNEWS of substance.

Luan Bexheti
Unnotable actor (?)

Neel Bhattacharya
Looks like a unotable actor.

Heather Blair
Not notable actress.

Calvin Blake III
Non-notable "up-and-coming" actor lacking GHits and GNEWS of substance.

Shelley Blond
Non-notable actress.

Elert Bode
Non-notable actor.

Holly Body
Non-notable porn actress.

Carson Bolde
Not a notable actor.

Nathan bond
Potentially non-notable actor (Google search only turns up namesakes).

Carly Bondar
Non-notable bit actress.

Elena Bondarchuk
Appears to be a non-notable actor who appeared in some TV shows.

Tera Bond
NN porn actress.

Richard Bonehill
Non-notable actor and stuntman.

Jack Boscoe
Non-notable child actor with only a single minor role (probably non-speaking) to his credit.

John Bosher
Up and coming actor/producer, but not sure if he's (yet) notable.

Carla Boudreau
Minor journeyman actress, earning a living playing bit/guest parts in those filmed-in-Vancouver low-budget productions.

Jack Bowman
Actor who has had many small roles, but nothing major.

Rupert Bradshaw
Actor of marginal notability.

Randall Brady
Non-notable actor.

Brianna Bragg
Non-notable pornographic actress.

Chloe Bridges
Unremarkable actress.

Hailey Bright
Not-notable actress.

Raven Brown
Minor actress, if an actress at all.

Robert Alan Browne
Minor actor with no significant roles in films, and only one minor role for 28 episodes of a TV soap opera.

Jennie Bruno
Jennie Bruno does not seem to pass the notability requirements for an actress.

Michael Budd
Non-notable actor and filmmaker.

Courtnie Bull
Former child actress who seems to be non notable who had only 3 roles total.

JJ Bunny
Non-notable actor lacking Ghits and GNEWS of substance.

Adam burke
Child actor who had a significant part in one film when he was 5 years old; nothing since.

Andrea burns
Non-notable actress.

Brandon Byrd
Non-notable actor with minimal credits.

Sam Byrne
Non-notable teen actor.

Lisa Ann Cabasa
Tv actress who basically all of her roles were just for a few episodes as minor characters.

Josh A. Cagan
Non-notable actor.

Luke Camilleri
Actor who has yet to achieve notability.

Helen Page Camp
Non-notable bit actress.

Ian Campbell
Non-notable actor.

Jon Campling
Non notable bit part actor.

Robin Camus
Actor with just one role.

Jason Cannon
Non-notable actor.

Recci Canon
Not a notable actor.

Bruce Carey
Non-notable actor.

Katherine Carlsberg
Seemingly unnotable actress.

Jaime Carroll
Non-notable actor.

Jack W. Carter
Non-notable actor.

Shawn Carter
Non-notable bit part actor.

John Carter
Non-notable actor.

Nicholas Cascone
Non-notable bit-part actor.

Mark Caso
non notable bit part actor

Erin Bethea Catt
Non-notable actress with two film credits.

Ashley Cavender-Jones
unotable actor.

Aziz Cem
Non-notable actor or martial artist.

Yin Chang
NN actress.

Sarah Charlotte
Apparently a non-notable actor, their most notable role being' Teenage Girl# 1' in a non-notable short.

Wylie Chiu
Minor actor lacking GHITs and GNEWS of substance.

Viorel Chivriga
Both Chivriga and Ciobanu are pretty minor actors on the Moldovan political scene: supporting players in the PAD, which is essentially a one-man show run by Mihai Godea.

Kavita Choudhary
Unotable actress.

Abhishek Chouksey
Non-notable 21 year old actor, director and hacker.

Elisa Christy
Non-notable actress.

Andy Clark
Not a notable actor.

Westcott Clarke
Non-notable actor who only had minor film roles

Jenn Colella
Not a notable actress.

Jerez coleman
Unremarkable actor / model / musician.

Jordyn Coleman
Non-notable actress with only a few minor roles to her credit.

Jessie Coleman
Non-notable actress.

Imelda Concepcion
Minor Filippino actress of the 50's

Jarlath Conroy
non-notable actor.

Araida Corbol
Non-notable actress.

Vladimir Correa
Unremarkable porn actor.

Peter Cowper
Unotable actor who is known for small roles.

Hilary Crane
Non-notable film actress.

Mimi Craven
Non-notable actress.

Ed Cray
Seems like a hard-working journeyman actor, but nothing establishes him as Notable.

Nikki Creswell
A non-notable actress.

Kenneth Paul Cruz (Filipino actor)
Notability questionable, just because he is the brother of one more well known actor doesn't make him notable.

Vladimir Cuk
Not sufficiently notable as an actor, athlete or entrepreneur.

Simon Curtis
Non notable actor.

Annalyn Cyrus
Non-notable actor.

Cherokee D'Ass
Non-notable porn actress.

Leila Danette
Non-notable minor actress who has played indignificant parts only (eg "Woman #2 in window"; four different parts in different episodes of a series).

Tanya Danielle
Doesn't seem to meet the standards for notability of a pornographic actor

Brittany Madelynn Daniels
Non-notable actor.

Ellie Darcey-Alden
An actor with 3 bit-parts in film and four TV episodes.

Joseph Darcey-Alden
An actor with one TV episode and one acting job in a 14-minute film.

Dani Dare
A non-notable child actor.

Petter Darin
Actor with questionable notability.

Jeremy Dash
Non-notable actor.

Dakota Daulby
An actor who is just starting out.

Eleanor David
Not notable as an actor.

Dean Davies
Actor who basically has only small parts and that's it.

Harrison C. Davies
Non-notable actor.

Ranie Daw
Non notable actress.

Deauxma
A pornographic actress whose
notability is contested.

Burr DeBenning
Non-notable actor.

Michelle DeFraites
Non-notable actor.

Vinny DeGennaro
Non-notable actor.

Jeffery Dench
Actor who is the brother of Dame
Judi Dench, but being related to a
notable person in itself confers no
degree of notability.

Brooke Devenney
Non-notable child actress.

Gina DeVettori
Non-notable actor.

Ihana Dhillon
Unotable actress with only one film
released so far.

George Dickerson
Non-notable washed up actor.

Danica Dillan
Not yet notable pornographic
actress.

Alana DiMaria
Non-notable actor lacking GHits
and GNEWS of substance.

Gianna Distenca
Non-notable actress.

Lucy Dixon
Probably non-notable actress.

Lucien Dodge
Non notable voice actor.

Bryan Domani
Actor who falls under too soon

Jason Donoghue
Non notable actor.

Lisa Donovan
Non notable internet actress.

Johnny Doran
Non-notable child actor, one
mention in the NYT's doesn't really
indicate a significant contribution
to the genre.

Cullen Douglas
Not a notable actor.

Eric Douglas
Unsuccessful actor and comedian
who happened to have been the son
of Kirk Douglas.

Penny Drake
Actress with only minor film roles.

Miglė Drąsutavičiutė
A former child actress who had lost
notability since her post-Kid Nation
stint.

Robbie Drebitt
Non notable actor.

Samantha Droke
non notable "bit part" actress

Burkely Duffield
As a child actor he only had a few
roles to his credit.

Angelina Duplisea
Actress who has only small parts in
very unknown films.

Nikita Dutta
Actress who seems to fall under
much too soon.

Alexander Cameron Dyer
Non-notable amateur actor.

Anne Dyson
Non-notable actress.

Odeen Eccleston
Actress with only minor roles in
TV and direct to DVD movie.

Andrea Edwards
Minor actress.

Lillian Eggers
Actress who was uncredited in half
a dozen films in a two year acting
period.

Margit Eklund
Non-notable actress.

Gabriel Ellis
Actor who once appeared in a 50
Cent film.

Brody emerson
Actor with only one very minor
role to his credit, in a film that
hasn't even been released yet.

Michael Epp
Non notable actor.

Julianna Erdesz
Erdesz is a non-notable model and
actress.

Ramon Estevez
Unimportant sibling to two famous
actors, Emilio Estevez and Charlie
Sheen.

Nicky Evans
Non-notable working actor.

Tyler Faith
Non notable porn actress, has done
nothing notable, doesn't appear to
have won any significant awards,
or started any new 'trends'

Blake Farris
Non-notable actor.

Alejandro Felipe
Actor has only had bit parts.

Joshua Ferdinand
Non-notable actor.

Kristyan Ferrer
Non-notable actor

Thor Fields
Non-notable actor/musician.

Nanci Filipelli
Model / Actress of no particular note.

Louis Findlay
minor actor, no notable roles

George Finn
Non-notable actor.

Perry Finnbogason
An actor who has had just had a few roles and was on a show for 5 episodes.

Ray Fisher
Not a notable actor

Simon Fisher-Becker
Entirely non-notable so-called actor.

Chrissie fit
Nonnotable actress.

Gabrielle Fitzpatrick
Non-notable actress.

Fob Five
A Google search for "Fob Five" brings up mostly submit-it-yourself video sites, and no mention of ever working with Amitabh Bachchan or other famous Bollywood actors....

Fernando De la Flor
Non-notable actor whose only appeared in one episode of one television show.

Alina Foley
Child actress with two roles, now unemployed because she was fired from Days after a month, nothing notable.

Nanna Fondo
Seems to be a non-notable actress.

Jim Ford
Non-notable, bit part actor.

Mark Foresta
A targetted Google for either the character or the actor produce no results.

Brandon Freiberg
Non-notable actor.

Jessa French
Television actress who has had small roles in various series.

Asako Fujii
Non-notable voice actor.

Becky Gable
There's no indication that she meets the notability criteria for martial artists or actors.

Maanvi Gagroo
Non notable actress with no really notable roles (okay it says one

staring role but that's it) rest are like "Crazed fan"

Bhavya Gandhi
Non notable Indian child actor

Toby Scott Ganger
Minor actor with no notability.

Samantha Garcia
Non-notable actor lacking GHits and GNEWS of substance.

Katie Garner
An actress that does not meet the notability requirements for actors and entertainers.

Taylor Garron
Non-notable child actor with no significant roles, the most notable being a contestant on FETCH!

Joey Gaydos
Not a notable actor.

Nathan Geist
No established notability as actor or soldier

David Geister
Non-notable actor lacking GHits and GNEWS of substance.

Max gell
Non-notable actor.

Tami-Adrian George
Non-notable actress with a series of minor roles.

Mary Gibbs
Non-notable child actress with 3 minor voice roles, only one of which is credited.

Bertie Gilbert
Child actor who had a very minor part in the last Harry Potter films.

George Giles
Non notable juvenile actor.

Alasdair Gillis
Unnotable former actor who appeared in a single series.

Seth Ginsberg
Non-notable bit part actor.

Maxwell Glick
A non-notable "actor".

Alésia Glidewell
Non-notable voice actor.

Ojas Godatwar
Un-notable actor.

Sage Goetz
Non-notable actor.

Cosette Goldstein
Non notable child actress

Julian Goncalves
A non notable actor/performer.

David Goodberg
Minor role actor & production assistant.

Tracy Goode
Virtually unknown actor outside of small roles in 3 Christian films.

Shalon Goss
Photographer (and aspiring actress) sister of notable artist Bryten Goss—does not seem to be notable on her own.

Mai Goto
Non-notable actress.

Aidan Gould
Unnotable child actor.

Nikhil Gowda
Non-notable actor with not even one released film to his name.

Kate Graham
Non-notable actor lacking GHits and GNEWS of substance.

Jamie Grant
Actress with questionable notability.

Sandra P. Grant
Non-notable actress who had a brief stint on one soap opera.

Maya Grant
Actress with very little indication of notability.

Léonor Graser
So far, Léonor Graser has not become notable as an academic either (as her professional activity seems to be as a lecturer at University of Paris III: Sorbonne Nouvelle and not as an actress).

Dee Green
Minor actress.

Jordan-Claire Green
Not a notable actress.

Spice Greene
non notable actor from non notable productions

J.J. Green
Actor who falls under too soon-all of his roles seem to be minor as well.

Jordan Greenhough
Non-notable actor.

Kelly Greyson
Non-notable actor lacking GHITS and GNEWS of substance.

Lara Grice
Bit part and extras actress, no major roles.

David Paul Grove
Small part actor.

Zabryna Guevara
Not a notable actress.

Michelle Guo
Not a notable actress or model.

Deepti Gupta
Non notable actress.

Prashantt Guptha
Non notable actor.

Fouad Habash
Non-notable actor with one role and no previous experience who starrred in a notable film.

Abby Hagyard
Unnotable actor.

Graham Haley
Non-notable actor and comedian.

Erika Hallberg
Non-notable actress.

Aaron Hamill
Non notable actor.

Wen Wen Han
Non-notable actress.

Happy (dog actor)
Are dog actors notable?

Dustin Harding
Is not (yet) a notable actor.

Johann Harmse
Actor with an amazing ONE performance!

Shane Harper
Kid actor sans any notable roles.

Tye Harper
Actor with VERY few unotable roles.

Gavin Harrison
Unnotable actor who played minor roles in a few films.

Nikki Harrup
Non-notable actress.

Frank Harts
Non-notable actor.

Lily Harvey
Non-notable child actor, hasn't appeared in anything yet, her casting in EastEnders has only just been announced.

Troy Hatt
Non-notable actor.

Cole Hawkins
Not a notable actor.

Prince hayer
Untoable actor

Zack Heart
Non-notable actor.

Kay Heberle
Non-notable actress.

Mari Henmi
Non-notable actress.

Eric Hennig
Non-notable actor with only uncredited or minor background parts.

Hank Henry
Non-notable actor.

Kate Henry
Actress who plays minor, mostly unnamed, characters.

Gregory J. Hepburn
Actor with questionable notability.

Maximiliano Hernández
Not a notable actor.

Socorro Herrera
NN actress who played an extremely minor role in High School Musical Malevious Userpage

Gavin Hetherington
Non-notable under-18 actor.

Ahmo Hight
Appears to be a non-notable actress/porn star

Arissa Hill
Non-notable reality TV contestant and aspiring "actress" and "singer"

William Daemon Hillin
nn actor/model/something.

Desi Arnez Hines II
Non-notable actor.

Ayumi Hodaka
A minor actress who only appeared in two TV series and one film based on one of those shows.

Kara and Shelby Hoffman
non-notable twin child actors with only 2 verifiable roles, as babies.

Thomas Hoffman
Non-notable actor.

Betty Lou Holland
She doesn't appear to have been that notable as an actress.

Jacqui Holland
Non-notable actress.

Roger Holloway
NN Actor.

Mazerinne Holskamp
Actress with only 1 role.

Natalie Hoover
Voice actress who has only had supporting roles in anime (even the ANN bolded roles such as Gargantia, Giovanni's Island, Fairy Fencer F, and Danganronpa 2 showed that even those roles were supporting/minor).

Thomas Howes
To date, a minor actor whose most notable part is a Second Footman. Actor of questionable notability

Clegg Hoyt
An actor with mostly minor roles; only one recurring TV role, as Mac in Dr. Kildare, and that only in six episodes.

Terrance Huff
Non-notable actor and filmmaker.

Hannah Hughes
Non-notable actor lacking non-trivial support.

Michael Conner Humphreys
Non-notable former child actor.

David Hunter
Non-notable actor: no major company or west end leads, one appearance in a television talent show, does not appear to have attracted any significant attention.

Patrick Hurd-Wood
Actor who has has had 3 minor roles in 3 films.

Wesley Ivan Hurt
Non-notable actor.

Aldo Huwyler
Actor who has just 2 roles that are not notable.

Henry Hübchen
An unnotable actor.

Hitomi Hyuga
An actress with just one role.

Holly Jack
Non notable actress only having one role in TV.

Robert Jacks
Non-notable actor.

Sarah Laurene Jackson
A non-notable model and actress.

Arol jahns
Non-notable actor.

Derrick James
Non-notable actor.

Kenneth W. James
Non-notable video-game voice actor.

Madison James
non-notable porn actress.

Radmar Agana Jao
Non-notable famous actor.

Bailey Jay
Non-notable adult film actress.

Jannike Kruse Jåtog
Non-notable Norwegian actress.

Jega
Insignificant actress actor not meeting general notability requirements

Luke Jeremy
Actor who falls under way too soon, he could be notable someday.

Avan Jogia
Non-notable actor.

Christy Johnson
An American actress and vocalist who sings for a non-notable band and appeared in a non-notable film has minor roles in film.

Michael Alan Johnson
Not a notable actor.

Nell Johnson
Actress with basically little notability.

Jay Armstrong Johnson
Non-notable actor

Rosin Jolly
Non-notable upcoming actor.

Alex Jones (child actor)
Child actor whose first tv show has not yet been released.

Brandon Jones
Completely unremarkable actor.

Stevie lynn jones
Non-notable teen actress.

Kandeyce Jorden
Non-notable actress/filmmaker/ artist.

Gayatri Joshi
The actress is only-known for her role in Swades and no signiificant amount of coverages found for it.

Jennifer Josy
Nonnotable actress; her IMDB listing shows only 5 bit parts.

Jacky Joy
Non-notable pornographic actress.

Jugnu ishiqui
Does not appear to be a notable actress (yet).

Farez Bin Juraimi
Actor who was in just one brief role and that's it.

Carlos Juvera
Minor actor.

Teanna Kai
Non-notable porno actress

Isabel Kaif
Sister of a notable actress Katrina Kaif but notability is not inherited.

Ron Kamoen
Actor is not notable.

Seerat Kapoor
Actress with only one role. - Too soon.

Zafar Karachiwala
Non-notable Indian actor; most notable English-language appearance seems to be as a minor, unnamed character in A Mighty Heart.

Adam Karst
Non-notable actor.

Dariush Kashani
Unremarkable minor actor.

Nhung Kate
Non-notable actress.

Satoshi Katougi
Non-notable voice actor.

George Katt
Non-notable minor actor

Sumela Kay
Not a notable actress.

Cary Alexander Kazemi
Non-notable actor; has played a handful of minor roles in non-notable films.

Andrew Keenan-Bolger
Non-notable actor.

Richardo Keens-Douglas
An actor who is most "known" for 2 small roles in 2 rather small films.

Christian Keiber
Non-notable actor.

Annette Betté Kellow
Non-notable actress and erotic dancer.

Beatrice Kelly
Non-notable actress.

Jacob Kemp
Minor actor with very little to show for--a minor part in a TV show, local repertory.

Roxanne Kernohan
Non-notable actress who has only had a few minor roles, nothing of any significance.

Donnie Keshawarz
Unremarkable actor.

Soumaya Keynes
Non-notable actress, related to notable people but not herself notable.

A. J. Khan
NN actress.

Prem Khan
Subject doesn't seem to have met notability criteria for an actor.

Khursheed Khan
Non-notable actor.

Keeya Khanna
Actress who falls under too soon.

Avantika Khattri
Unotable actress with just 2 roles so far.

Michelle Kim
Non-notable actress.

Meade Kincke
Non notable actor.

Rebecca Kiser
Actress with very questionable notability, none of her films seem to be that notable yet either

Camryn Kiss
non-notable pornographic actress.

Natasha Kizmet
Non-notable actress lacking GHits and GNEWS of substance.

Oğuzhan Koç
Actor with only a few roles, nothing significant either.

Matt Kohler
Non-notable actor.

Aditya Kohli
Actor who has had minor roles in two films.

Kim Komatsu
Minor actress with no notability.

Saki Kondo
Minor actress who only appeared in two TV shows and one film.

Illya Konstantin
Non-notable actor lacking GHits and GNEWS of substance to support notability.

Jon Krampner
Non-notable actor.

Bruce Kronenberg
Non-notable voice actor/actor.

Yuvraj Kumar
non-notable actor.

Amala Rose Kurian
Actress with just one role so far.

Polina Kuzminskaya
Unotable actress with unotable roles only.

Aaron Michael Lacey
Seems to be a non-notable actor, pretty much all roles uncredited or very minor.

Hashim Lafond
Apparently minor actor, with his supposedly best-known-for roles including "Carnival Patron" and "Student".

Anthony Lambert-Whitford
Hmm, seems not notable (an extra) - but has starred next to a big actor in a film.

Mitchell Landzaat
Non-notable actor, he played minor roles such as cops, a helmsman and a handyman in TV movies/mini-series according to IMDB.

Eric Lane
NN actor.

Jayme Langford
A non-notable pornographic actress.

Mary Lanier
Non-notable actress.

Mike Lapointe
Non notable actor.

Cristina Lark
Non-notable actor lacking ghits and Gnews.

Rebecca Larsen
Non-notable actor lacking GHits and GNEWs of substance.

Bartell LaRue
Non-notable voice actor.

Kenyon Lasseter
Non-notable minor actor with a small part in one TV episode.

Trent Latta
Formerly an unnotable actor with a few bit part roles, now an unnotable attorney.

Michael St. Laurent
Non-notable drag queen and actor; only acting credit is bit-part in the The Rose as female impersonator.

Syr Law
Non-notable actor lacking Ghits and GNEWS of substance.

Lexi Lawson
Not a notable actress.

Derek Lea
Non-notable bit-part actor.

Kennedy Leigh
Non-notable porn actress.

Melissa Leigh
Actress who is of borderline notability.

Dustin James Leighton
NN actor - a bunch of bit parts and voice-over work.

Linda Leonard
Non-notable Funimation voice actor.

Jason Leung
Non-notable actor

Brian Levinson
Levinson was a run of the mill child actor from age 10 to 15.

Melanie Liburd
Minor actor lacking non-trivial support.

Evelyn Lin
Non-notable pornographic actress.

Ryan Lindsay
Non-notable actor.

Kurt Lockwood
Non-notable porno actor.

Thomas James Longley
Non-notable actor.

Chad Lopez
Non-notable actor.

Francisco Lorite
Non notable actor/writer/director.

Peter Losasso
Actor who has only appeared in two episodes (per IMDb) of a show that's not exactly burning up the airwaves yet.

Kia Luby
Non-notable actor.

Benjamin W.S. Lum
Non-notable actor.

Willie Macc
Non notable comedian and actor.

Richard Madden
Non-notable actor.

Luka Magnotta
Non-notable model/porn actor.

V. Mahadevan
Tamil actor who does not appear notable.

Jarrett Maier
Non-notable actor lacking non-trivial support.

Vishal Malhotra
Non-notable Indian actor appearing in a minor television roles.

Pawan Rama Mali
Actor of doubtful notability.

Catherine Manett
Non-notable actress.

Tawnya Manion
Non-notable fanfilm actress.

Edward Mannix
Minor voice actor.

Samuel Marcus
Actor is not a minor.

Tom Mariano
Not notability, "Actor" plays only uncredited roles.

Bailey Markum
Non-notable actor.

Irene Marot
Relatively minor British television actor; unable to find enough press to demonstrate notability.

Tia Marrie
Not a notable actress.

Isaac Marshall
Unnotable voice actor.

Deena Martin
Non-notable actress - no major roles, awards, etc.

Meaghan Jette Martin
Minor (in more ways than one) actress, whose only significant role was a made-for-cable movie, 5th-billed.

Marcella Martin
Non-notable actress that had a minor role in one significant film.

Ricky Martinez
Non-notable porn actor.

Philippe Martin IV
Actor whose roles are all really obscure and no notability.

Tara Mason
Canadian actress with three minor (extra) film roles.

Grazielli Massafera
Brazilian actress with just two works on brazilian TV.

Danny Mastrogiorgio
Non-notable actor.

Sarah Beck Mather
Non-notable actress.

Connor Matheus
Non-notable television actor.

Bernie Matthew
Non-notable actor.

Johan Matton
Non notable actor

Joe Maw
Child actor who seems to have received no press attention for his role in Tracy Beaker Returns.

Ange Maya
Non-notable actress lacking GHits of substance and zero GNEWS.

Julie Mayfield
She's a voice actress for Funimation, but does not have any major lead roles in any shows.

Jirina Mazankova
non-notable pornographic actress.

Jynx Maze
non-notable pornographic actress for now.

Jeff Mazzola
Non notable actor, producer and prop master.

Debra Lynne McCabe
Doesn't seem to be that notable of an actress.

Deborah McCallum
Patently non-notable actress.

Jay McCarey
Non-notable actor.

Angel McCord
Non-notable actress.

Rocky McCord
Non-notable actor.

Nichi McFarlane
Non-notable actress with no major credits.

Norman McGuire
nn actor, played bit parts in a few
TV shows.

Elizabeth Mclaughlin
Non-notable actress who was in
one straight-to-video movie and
had a bit part on a single episode of
Ugly Betty.

Jason C. McLean
Non-notable actor.

Christopher McLinden
Non-notable actor.

Suzie McSnuzie
No google hits for supposed actor;
likely fictional.

Jack Meakin
Non-notable actor.

Derek Mears
Minor actor and stunt man.

Nevin Meçaj
An actor with just one film that
was back in 2001.

Curt Mega
Non-notable bit-part actor.

Dana Melanie
Non-notable actor lacking ghits and
Gnews of substance.

Elizabeth Melendez
Not a notable actress.

Sofia Mendez
Non-notable actress.

Lucy Merriam
Non-notable 7 year old actress.

Ryan Metcalf
Obscure actor with just a few roles.

Cherie Michan
Actress who does not meet the
basic notability requirements.

Jessica Mila
Model and actress.

Nevin Millan
Actor/producer with no major roles
in a notable production, nor any
awards for short films.

Matt Millburn
Non-notable minor actor.

Addy Miller
Non-notable actor.

Omar Benson Miller
A minor-bit actor.

Andrew Mills
Non-Notable actor, who has only
appeared in 4 underground horror
films all produced in the past year.

Alex Miranda
Non-notable actor/film industry
personality.

Atticus Mitchell
Actor with questionable notability.

Hugh Mitchell
Non-notable child actor - only two minor roles in two major films.

Ayesha Mohan
Non Notable actress.

Melissa Monet
Non-notable porn actress and director.

Zoey Monroe
A non-notable porn actress.

Karlie Montana
Non-notable pornographic actress.

Harry Monty
An actor with many roles, but they are all minor.

Robert Moon
Non-notable actor and improvisation instructor.

Leonora Moore
Non-notable actress.

Liz Moses
Non-notable actress, only two very minor roles since 1980.

Danny Mountain
Non-notable porn actor.

Kelsey Mulrooney
Non-notable actress with a single minor role in a film and some minor TV appearances.

Javier Muñoz
Not a notable actor.

Mark Murphy
Does not appear to be a notable actor.

Nina Muschallik
Non-notable actress.

Donny Myers
Non-notable U.S. theatrical actor.

Stacee Myers
Non-notable actor lacking non-trivial support.

Griffin Myers
obscure or unknown actor

Branden Nadon
Actor with only a few non notable roles.

Chikayo Nakano
Non-notable actor with one supporting role in Madlax.

Eri Nakao
Japanese voice actor with a bunch of supporting roles in anime shows, but difficult to find any lead roles in major productions.

Jason Narvy
Non-notable actor has never
done anything other than Power
Rangers.

Suzanna von Nathusius
She is not a notable child actor.

Melissa Navia
Non-notable actress.

Sean Needham
Non-notable actor, if actor at all.

John Neilson
Non-notable actor who had a
couple of bit parts in a handful of
memorable films.

Kristin Nelson
Not notable as an actor or painter.

Ben-Jamin Newham
Non-notable actor.

Pauline Newstone
Non-Notable voice actor.

Obilo Ng'ongo
Not-notable actor.

Nick Nichols
Unnotable Canadian actor.

Lisa Niemi
An actress who seems to be notable
only for being Patrick Swayze's
wife.

Nischal
Non-notable film actor with lots of
completely unsupported assertions.

Nissae Isen
Non-notable voice actress.

Vishaal Nityanand
Non-notable actor / filmmaker.

Kathryn Noble
a b-movie actress with just 2 roles.

Sonia Noemí
non-notable actress

Michael De Nola
nn actor with half a dozen film
parts, either bit parts in major
films, or parts in bit films, and a
couple of TV appearances.

Tara Nulty
Non-notable actress with no major
credits or awards.

Joshua O'Brien
A non-notable bit part television
actor.

Daniel O'Connor
Unsuccessful contestant on
Australian Idol, and now a bit-part
actor on Australian soap-opera.

Seregon O'Dassey
Actress without major roles or
press buzz.

Oliver O'Dea
Does not meet notability criteria
for actors.

April O'Neil
AVN award (twitter queen) not
significant award and XBIZ award
(girl/girl actress) scene related.

Chris O'Neil (comedian)
Non-notable bit actor.

Sundra Oakley
Non-notable actress and reality TV
show contestant.

Izumi Ogami
Voice actress only notable for one
supporting role in Inuyasha.

Mariko Okubo
Non-notable actor lacking non-
trivial support.

Shunsuke Okubo
Actor in minor roles, mostly in
minor movies.

Vince Orlando
Unremarkable actor/screenwriter.

Joshua Ormond
Non-notable actor lacking non-
trivial support.

Ash Ortega
Unotable actress who has yet to get
stardom

Alexia Osborne
Actress with just a single credit in
an as yet unreleased film.

Ed Oxenbould
Not a notable actor.

Mizuki Ōtsuka
Non-notable voice actor.

Dener Pacheco
He has just a few experience as an
actor.

Laurel Page
Non-notable voice actress.

Jordan Palmer
Non-notable actor.

Rajendra panchal
Does not appear to be a notable
theater actor.

Panky
Actor who has very little notability

Calen Maiava Paris
Non-notable actor.

Tammy Parks
Non-notable pornographic
(softcore) actress.

Suraj Partha
Non-notable actor.

Mitesh Kumar Patel
Non-notable actor/producer lacking
GHits of substance and GNEWS.

Henry Patterson
Non-notable actor.

Namik Paul
Non-notable actor lacking non-trivial support.

Ahti Paunu
nn actor and singer.

Raegan Payne
Non-notable actress.

Hunter Pecunia
Non-notable child actor.

Quran Pender
Non-notable actor.

Loreto Peralta
Does not appear to be a notable actor.

Carmen Perez
Non-notable actress.

Brittany Perrineau
Not a notable actress.

Biju Phukan
A non-notable actress.

Reba Phukan
A non-notable actress.

Justin Pickett
A minor actor with no significant roles (he has had guest appearances on multiple show - usually for only one episode).

Sarah Pickthall
Actress known for just one kids show and that's it.

Perri Pierre
Non-notable actor.

Pile (voice actress)
Some Random actress who was an amazing ONE role and some CDs.

Caroline Pires
Irrelevant actress never did anything notable.

Jack Polick
Unremarkable actor.

Preechaya Pongthananikorn
Non-notable actress.

Laura Post
Amateur actress known for fan projects.

Eric Potts
Appears to be unremarkable actor and TV extra.

Thomas Price
Non-notable actor lacking GHits and GNEWS of substance.

Florence Pugh
Actress who falls under too soon.

Haley Alexis Pullos
Non-notable teen actress

Brian Pumper
completely non-notable actor.

Christopher Purdy
Non-notable actor, only credit was a short from six years ago.

Amjad J. Qaisen
Non-notable actor.

Julian Quintart
A actor who has done only non notable roles.

Damaine Radcliff
Actor who's role are minor in nature.

Elijah Ramos
Non professional aspiring actor

Roxie Ramos
Non-notable actress...

Randy Raney
Actor that played minor roles in two films.

Emad raouf
non-notable actor

Roxy Rare
Non-notable porn actress; has appeared in several movies but has garnered no awards or other mention to establish notability.

Mishon Ratliff
Non-notable actor

Cecile Raubenheimer
Non-notable actress with some minor roles, who appears to be working in the hotel trade.

Kane Raven
Non notable actor.

Charlie Ray
Non-notable actress.

Tiffany Rayne
Non-notable pornographic actress.

Reza Razavi
Non-notable actor.

Faye Reagan
Non-notable porn actress.

Emily Grace Reaves
Non-notable child actress.

Bettina Redlich
NN actress.

Aaron Refvem
Non-notable child actor.

Lisa Regina
Seems to be a non-notable actress.

Richard Alan Reid
Minor actor lacking GHits and GNEWs of substance.

Sebastian Reid
Minor actor lacking GHits and GNEWS of substance.

JM Reyes
Non-notable minor actor.

Sammie Rhodes
Non-notable porn actress.

Craig Richards
Non notable actor.

Brandōn Richardson
Seems to be a non-notable actor.

Prince Richardson
Actor of no detectable notability.

Armando Riesco
Non-notable working actor.

Noah Ringer
Actor has only appeared in two films.

Leslie Garza Rivera
Mexican actress with no notable roles.

Martin Roach
Non-notable actor.

Emily Robins
Non notable actress that has a minor role in a Soap opra.

Sheldon F. Robins
Actor, writer, producer who is non-notable.

Samuel Robinson
Non-notable actor.

Geneviève De Rocray
Dubbing actress who has very little amount of roles (outside of doing the dubbing voice for princess Jasmine, can't find much else notability)

Vicky Rodewyk
Non-notable actress.

Ron Rogge
An actor with no indications of notability.

Curt roland
Non-notable minor actor.

Chelsea Romero
non-notable pornographic actress.

Walter Romney
Non-notable actor.

Ilza Rosario
Actress and singer who does not appear to be notable yet, despite one role in the movie Burn Notice.

Mick Del Rosario
Appears to be a not-yet-notable actor.

Croc Rose
May lack notability as an actor.

Daphne Rosen
Does not meet notability for Pornographic actors and models, she never won an award (only was in a movie that won), only

nominated once for an award,
has not unique contributions to a
specific pornographic genre, etc

Sofia Rosinsky
Child actor with only minor roles.

Avy Lee Roth
Non-notable porn actress.

Nick Roux
Minor actor who is not notable.

Cody Rowlett
Non-notable actor.

Briana Roy
Non-notable actress.

Vipul Roy
Non-notable actor lacking GHits
and GNEWS of substance.

Masum Parvez Rubel
Non-notable as actor or martial
artist.

Natalie Rushman
An actress that does not appear to
have any notability.

Geoffrey Russell
Minor British television actor;
can't find any significant press to
indicate notability.

Lee Wayne Ryder
Non-notable actor.

Joseph Rye
Non-notable actor.

Hussan Saad
Actor with just a few roles so far
which falls under the too soon
criteria.

Nishikant Sadaphule
Non-notable actor/director.

Brodie Sanderson
Non-notable actor.

Nanami Sano
A voice actress with just one role.

Ayana Sasagawa
Non-notable voice actor.

Sarang Sathaye
Actor with only a few unotable
roles

Manolita Saval
Non-notable actress.

Manuel Saval
Non-notable actor.

Ashley Sawdaye
Non-notable or marginally notable
actor.

Verushka Scalia
Likely non-notable actress.

Tom Schanley
non notable actor.

Cameron Scher
very minor child actor.

Marion Scherer
non notable actress with only very
minor roles

Scott Schiaffo
non notable actor

Amy and Zoe Schlagel
Apparently non-notable actresses
whose roles have been confined to
bit parts to date.

Lenny Schmidt
non-notable actor

Michael Q. Schmidt
Minor character actor, with no real
prominent roles.

Jumbo Schreiner
German actor who does not seem
notable even in German-speaking
countries.

Aaron Schwartz
Non-notable actor

Maïté Schwartz
Non notable actress

Gary Schwartz
Actor is not notable.

James Scott Irving
Non-notable actor.

Jocelyn Seagrave
Non-notable actress.

Adam Searles
Non notable former child actor who
now has a few bit parts in British
TV series to his credit.

Aima Rosmy Sebastian
Non-Notable Malayalam actress

Anya Selecki
Non-notable actress lacking Ghits
and GNews of substance.

Scott Sewperman
Non notable pornographic actor
with a role in only one film.

Josh Shada
Actor who has only appeared an
very minor roles.

Dimple Shah
Non notable actress, no outstanding
roles

Heeba Shah
Non notable actress.

Farhad Shahnawaz
Actor best known for a relatively
minor role.

Martin Shakar
American actor with no notable
roles.

Kunal Sharma
actor who falls under too soon, none of his films are out yet, now someday, but not yet.

Jimmy Shaw
Non-notable actor.

Sandra Shaw
Non-notable bit actress.

David Shea
nn actor/model.

Angela V. Shelton
Non-notable actress.

Susie Shinner
Actress whose only credit to date was cut from the film.

Sachin Shivalia
Unremarkable actor.

Naga shourya
Non-notable Telugu actor.

Umeka Shōji
Non-notable voice actor.

Ankita Shrivastava
Non notable actress, had small stints in the movies.

Seth Sieunarine
Minor TV actor, no starring roles anywhere.

Sandeep Sikand
Actor with just 3 non notable roles.

Jon Simanton
Non-notable actor.

Jenna Rose Simon
Non-notable minor actor lacking non-trivial support.

Ted Simonett
Non-notable bit actor.

Ty Simpkins
Non-notable child actor with a few minor roles.

Jeanmarie Simpson
Subject does not pass the notability standards for actors or activists.

Tony Deon Sims
An actor.

Aditi Singh
Actress with no notability to be found - she has done no films as of now, so way too soon.

Lakha Lakhwinder Singh
Non notable actor.

Deepak Singh
Non-notable actor.

Jigyasa Singh
Non-notable actress.

Derek Sitter
Bit part actor.

Beth Skipp
Non-notable actress.

Jesse Smith, Jr.
Not notable as an actor or martial
artist.

T. Ryder Smith
Non-notable actor/actress

Katlynn Simone Smith
Non-notable actress.

Riley Smith
Non-notale actor and singer.

Ron Smoorenburg
Notability as an actor or martial
artist not established.

Alexandra Socha
NN replacement actress in a
Broadway musical

Meilinda Soerjoko
Actress with too few and minor
credits.

Michael Soll
An actor/screenwriter known for a
VERY obscure film.

Ari Sorko-Ram
Fails notability as an actor and for
general notability

Gus Sorola
Being a computer technician and
voice actor is not enough, not by a
far stretch.

Bill Sorvino
Actor/film festival owner who has
won only local awards and appears
to have only local notability.

Ed Spear
Not notable; an actor with only one
role.

Melissa Spell
Actress with a small handful
of roles, apparently as a minor
character or extra.

Vanessa Spencer
Non-notable actress.

Joseph Stacey
Non-notable actor.

Jonna Leigh Stack
An actress who just has one role.

Connor Stanhope
Non-notable child actor.

Charmane Star
Non-notable porno actress.

Carrie Stauber
Carrie Stauber is a non-notable
actress.

Kate Steavenson-Payne
Non-notable actress.

Laurie Steele
Voice actor whose only major role
was young Krillin in the Dragon
Ball series.

Elena Stejko
Non-notable actress with only minor parts.

Kaj Stenberg
Non-notable actor.

Joulia Stepanova
Non-notable acress or perhaps just non-verifiably notable actress.

Samantha Sterlyng
Appears to be a non-notable porn actress.

Bert L. Stevens
Non-notable actor who seemed to be an "extra" in many films in the 1940s-1960s.

Stuart Stevens
Non-notable actor.

Lara Stevens
Appears to be a non-notable porn actress.

Sean Ali Stone
Non-notable actor.

Malcolm Storry
Not a notable actor.

Stuart Styron
Non-notable as actor, musician, or artist.

Yuna Sugiyama
Child actress who seems to fall under too soon-someday she probably will deserve her own page-but not yet.

Sumbul Iqbal
Non-notable actor, mentioned only in a couple of blogs.

Clinton Sundberg
Non-notable actor.

Thesy Surface
Non-notable actress.

Eliska Sursova
Non-notable actress.

Buddy Swan
Minor actor in a major film.

Eliza Swenson
Non-notable actress and producer, mainly of direct-to-video productions or in minor roles.

Natsuki Takahashi
Minor actress with a short career who only appeared on 3 TV shows and had no significant film roles.

Satoshi Taki
Non-notable voice actor.

Mia Talerico
Non-notable child actress who, according to IMDb, has been on one episode of a TV show.

Steve Talmud
Non-notable actor

Talon
Non-notable porno actor.

Natasha Talonz
Non-notable actress.

Dijon Talton
Not a notable actor.

Jason Tam
Not a notable actor.

Jasmine Tame
Not notable under pornographic actress criteria.

Felicia Tang
Non-notable actress/model.

Megumi Tano
Non-notable voice actor.

Tara
Non-notable actress, has never appeared in any notable films.

Clayton Taylor
Non-notable actor.

Isis Taylor
Taylor is a throughly undistinguished pornographic film actor.

Cat Tebo
Unremarkable actress whose only credits to date are future releases.

Obi Tenaka
Non-notable singer or actor.

Aaron Thomas
NN actor.

Joe J Thomas
Non-notable voice actor (most of his career seems to be fairly minor roles).

Prentiss Thompson
Minor actor of no particular notability.

Saige Thompson
Non-notable actress.

Ben Thornton
Non-notable child actor, has a few minor credits.

Mike Timoney
Non-notable actor.

Kanika Tiwari
Child actress who has had one low-credited role.

Haley Tju
Non-notable child actress.

Jordan Todosey
Non-notable actress.

Klebber Toledo
Minor actor lacking GHits and GNews of substance.

Varun Toorkey
Unotable actor with just a couple roles.

Kira Tozer
Non-notable voice actress.

Michael Treanor
Child actor, with no major roles.

Andrew Trischitta
Non-notable minor actor lacking Ghtis and GNEWS of substance.

Rati Tsiteladze
Non-notable athlete, actor and model.

Dylan Turner
Non-notable actor/singer.

Melanie Kay Turner
Non-notable actress.

Brian Tyler
Non-notable actor.

Donier Tyler
Non-notable actress.

Tsubee U
Actress which fails to meet the notability requirements for actors.

Alban Ukaj
Actor who is basically in a bunch of unotable roles.

Billy Unger
Non-notable child actor.

Meryem Uzerli
Actress that played minor roles only in several films.

Roland Varno
Actor with no indications of notability.

Vishal Vashishtha
Unotable actor with just a couple of roles.

Tanvi Verma
An actress with just 2 unotable roles.

Chloe Vevrier
Non-notable pornographic model and former actress.

Craig Vincent
nn working actor, just no external notability

Vinny De Vingo
Non-notable actor and producer.

Trishna Vivek
Indian TV actress.

Rashidah De Vore
Actress with only a couple unotable roles so far.

Gloria Votsis
Non-notable actress.

Raphaël W.Pathé
non-notable actor.

Shelley Waggener
Non-notable actress, with appearances in bit parts of various films and TV shows.

Sara Wakatsuki
Actor known mainly for one role as Asuna in the live-action Negima series.

Kim Wakerman
not notable not a famous actor not even on imdb unlike Bel Powley

Oliver Walker
Non notable actor with small appearance in movies.

Patricia Walker
Non-notable actress who was married to Blake Edwards.

Braden Walkes
Child actor, but not notable yet.

A.J. Walsh
Non-notable actor.

Mark Walton (story artist)
Unnotable story artist and minor voice actor.

Ryan Ward
Non-notable actor.

Luke Ward-Wilkinson
Non-notable child actor - ghits reveal minimal mentions or short/ empty filmographies at mtv.com, imbd, tv.com, youtube, blogs etc.. etc.

Tashiana Washington
Insufficiently notable actor.

Mollie Weaver
Unnotable voice actress in the English dubs of a small handful of anime series, primarily minor parts.

Roman Weaver
Seemingly non-notable actor.

Lucy Webb (British actor)
A young actor, who unfortunately is not notable enough for inclusion.

Ben Weinberger
Non notable actor

Brad Charlton Wells
non-notable actor, only role is unreleased

Carlucci Weyant
Non-notable model and actor.

Kit Weyman
Subject does not appear to be notable, either as an actor or a rapper.

Andi Whaley
Minor voice actress.

Layla and Logan Wheeler
Young actors, not notable enough for inclusion.

George Wienbarg
Non-notable actor/broadcaster.

Rob Wiethoff
Non-notable actor.

Don Wilbanks
Non-notable actor who seems to have never made it above extra work.

Steve Will
Non-notable actor.

Athelston Williams
Non-notable actor, famous only for an injoke.

Toby Williams
British actor with a career full of unimpressive roles, and a comedian who is apparently "award winning", but it is unclear what award he has won.

Tyrel Jackson Williams
Non-notable minor actor lacking GHits and GNEWS of substance.

Pete Williams
Unotable voice actor

Ben Alekzsander Williams
A non notable bit part actor and band member.

Scot Williams
Non-notable actor.

Daniel Williams
Non-notable actor.

Tim Wilson (filmmaker)
Non-notable actor lacking Ghits and GNEWS of substance.

Beth Winslet
Non-notable actress, who hasn't done many roles in notable features.

John T. Woods
Non-notable actor.

Melissa Jean Woodside
Non-notable actor.

Derrick Worsley
Not a notable actor.

Deborah Worthing
Non-notable actress.

Rick Worthy
non-notable actor.

Stephen Wozniak
Non-notable actor.

Alexander Wraith
Non-notable actor - notability not supported.

Sophie Wu
Non-notable actress.

Martin Wuttke
Non-notable actor.

David Wyles
Non-notable actor.

May Wynn
An actress with only one major film credit (The Caine Mutiny) and only as a supporting character.

Alyssa & Hannah Yadrick
Young actors, not notable enough
for inclusion.

Kotomi Yamakawa
Non-notable voice actor whose
most prominent role was Ako in
Negima which was not one of the
major characters in the series.

Barry Yandell
Funimation voice actor but all his
roles are supporting to minor ones,
so it is not clear what he is most
notable for and why he should stay
around.

Chingmy Yau
Non-notable inactive actor.

Eser Yenenler
Yet ANOTHER unotable actor with
just a few roles.

Hakan Yildiz
Non-notable actor lacking GHits
and GNEWS of substance.

Lindsay Younce
Non-notable "actress" who
appeared in one religious film in
2004 and has since disappeared.

America Young
Non-notable voice actress.

Gerard Christian Zacher
Unknown actor.

Zafira
No indication that any of the
notability criteria for pornographic
actors and models are met.

Seemi Zaidi
Seems to be a unotable actress.

David K. Zandi
Actor with a total of two
(uncredited) roles at imdb, and
supposedly a producer too but imdb
has nothing.

Salar Zarza
Non-notable actor lacking in-depth
secondary support.

Animator

Ethan Atwood
Non notable animator who falls
under too soon.

Timothy Bailey
Unremarkable animator.

Colbert Fennelly
Non-notable effects animator.

Jen Kamerman
Unremarkable animator with small
career on one show.

Clay Kaytis
Non-notable animator lacking
GHits and GNEWS of substance.

Garry Lewis
Apparently a working artist, but
no major exhibitions, etc. How
many 3D animators are there in the
industry, anyhow?

David Lovelace
Non notable animator.

Mark Marek
Seemingly unnotable animator.

Lance Wilder
Non-notable animator.

Architect

Sheba Akhtar
Appears to be non-notable Pakistani architect and writer.

William Ransom (Bill) Campbell
Non-notable architect lacking non-trivial support.

Shaahin Espahbodi
non-notable architect.

Mark Hackett
Architect from Northern Ireland, but all of the awards and achievements are attributable to the company Hackett Hall McKnight, of which he is one partner.

Jan Klerks
NonNotable architect.

Carl O. Nordling
Non-notable Scandinavian architect.

Paul preissner
Unremarkable architect.

J.F. Reynolds
Local architect with no wide notability

Sami Rintala
Architect of somewhat lacking notability.

Serge Schoemaker
Looks like a promising young architect, but not notable yet (no major building, no major publication, no major award).

Barbara Ellen Waxman
From what can be found, the individual is just a typical lawyer and architect with no significant accomplishments.

Author

Walid Abdallah
Non-notable author.

John Christian Abrahamson
Non-notable author lacking non-trivial support.

Curtis Ackie
Non-notable author lacking GHITS and GNEWS of substance.

Christina Adams
Questionable notability of a writer/producer of three movies.

Lavonne Jayne Adams
Non-notable author lacking GHits and GNEWS of substance.

Nick Adams (political author speaker)
Non notable author: 2 self published books, on iuniverse, which worldcat shows is almost no library.

Koji Aihara
Non-notable author of Even a Monkey Can Draw Manga.

Shamal Akrayi
Poet of unclear notability.

John Albrecht Jr.
Non-notable author.

Raymond Allan
Non-notable author of a single fiction book for teens.

Rasheed bin Mohammad Altokhi
Writer of questionable notability.

Mary Francis Ames
Non-notable children's book author.

Cleveland Amory
Non notable author.

Ananthu
Non-notable Indian screenplay writer.

Melinda Anderson
Author apparently notable for one book only.

Nick Aplin
Non-notable academic and author

Chris Armold
Author of a number of somewhat obscure books.

Sydenham Arts
Author deprodded.

P. M. H. Atwater
Not a notable author.

Rassool Russell Auckbaraullee
Non-notable self-published author.

Carina Axelsson
Non notable author, has 3 books published by vanity presses.

Lee Bacon
Potentially non-notable author.

Lyn bagnall
Non notable author and gardening expert.

T.N. Baker
Apparently non-notable author.

Farooq Bakshi
Non-notable poet.

Doug Baldwin
non notable writer.

Martin bamford
Barely known author, hardly meets notability criteria.

Subhro Bandyopadhyay
Non notable poet.

Rashidul Bari
Non notable author.

Dan Barnabic
Non-notable activist and author.

Perry Belcher
Non-notable author with a few self-published books under his belt.

Manikanta Belde
Non-notable author.

Celia Berrell
Non-notable writer/poet.

Dean Bertram
Little known as a director or as a freelance writer.

Bob Black (comedy writer)
Non-notable writer, does not appear to have won any awards or contributed unique work to his genre.

David Blacker
Author which won one minor award for one book.

Ryan Blacketter
non notable author.

Kerry Blair
Writer who has no notability established.

Marcus Blake
Non notable author.

David Blixt
Non notable author: only 1 book with more than 2 library holdings.

Jonathan Blum
Non notable author of a single non notable book.

Kathryn Borel Jr.
Non-notable author.

Timothy Boronczyk
Apparently non-notable author.

Lassy Bouity
Non-notable author.

Les Branson
Unpublished poet/novelist; non-notable indy filmmaker.

Annette Breaux
Non-notable author.

Laurence B. Brown
Author of non notable self published books.

Sir Mark Bruback
NN poet.

Rob Bryanton
Not notable as a composer or an author.

Jae Bryson
Non-notable author.

Stephen Burge
Non-notable comedy writer

George Burk
nn air crash survivor, author, speaker.

Alexander C.Morley
Non-notable self-published writer.

Olivia Fox Cabane
The author of a single book is not notable separately from the book.

Rob Cabitto
Non notable author.

Steven Callahan
Non-notable person, author of non-notable book.

Mayra Calvani
Non-notable writer.

Abby Campbell
Non-notable author of a single book that has not yet been released (according the author's own spec sheet).

Patrick Carman
nn author; his books rank 37,309th (Into the Mist), 53,593rd (Tenth City), 109,590th (Beyond the Valley of Thorns), 55,554th (House of Power), and 367,520th (Dark Hills Divide) in sales at Amazon.com

Fern G.Z. Carr
Non-notable poet lacking GHits and GNEWS of substance.

Vednita Carter
Not a notable author or activist.

John Caslin
Likely non-notable author.

Nick Catalano
Non-notable author/academic.

Steven M. Cerutti
Non-notable author and professor.

Bryce Chandler
Non-notable self-published author.

Belinda Chang
Appears to be non-notable Chinese writer.

Mark Charlesworth
Non-notable author of self-published poetry books and a novel published by self-publishing firm Hirst Books

Daniel Churchill
Notability has not been established as a chef, an author, or a TV performer.

Andrew Clarke
Non-notable author lacking GHits and GNEWS of substance.

Augusta Clawson
Non-notable author, only gets 80 Google hits.

Tom Cohen
Unremarkable academic and author.

Sebastian Cole
Non-notable author lacking Ghits and GNews of substance.

Brandon Collier
Non-notable author.

Greg Colton
Non-notable television writer.

Jethro Compton
apparently unpublished as writer.

Glenn Cooper
Non-notable author

Philip Coppens
Non-notable author.

Edwin Cordevilla
Non-notable poet.

Susie Cornfield
Non-notable author.

Brian J. Costello
Non-notable author.

Maurice Cotterell
Not a notable author.

Pamela Cox
Non-notable children's author.

Cleo Coyle
Non-notable author.

Joseph Crisalli
Self-published author of questionable notability.

Alistair Cross
Non-notable author.

Jason Crummey
He is an unelected candidate and not a notable writer.

White Crusade
Non-notable author, non-notable publisher, no reviews, and nothing resembling an RS.

Joan Carroll Cruz
Non-notable author.

Carrie Cuinn
Non-notable author lacking GHits and GNews of substance.

Jonathan Culver
Apparently non-notable self-published author.

Daniel Cure
Author whose only work is the self-published book The Road to Inherita[nce], from vanity press Trafford Publishing.

Cuvie
Un-notable author.

Vasant Abaji Dahake
Non notable poet.

Ellen Kristin Dahl-Pedersen
Apparently non-notable author.

Bigyan Darshan
A 17-year old Nepali poet and social worker.

Sanjoy Das
Non notable poet.

Minakshi Datta
Non notable author.

Richard Daughty
Non-notable writer.

Rainye Day
Does not meet the notability criteria for authors or the general notability criteria.

Alexander DeLuca
Non-notable blogger and author of a self-published book.

Manilal Desai
Non notable writer.

Alain Dizerens
Non-notable author.

Joseph Dobrian
Unremarkable feelance writer and unsuccessful fringe mayoral candidate.

Billie J. Dominick-Cooper
Non-notable poet.

André Douzet
A somewhat obscure French author.

James Downey (Internet performance artist)
Author of two self-published books, neither of which gained much attention.

Hasan Draei
Not notable writer, author of only one book, which is not notable either.

Zebulon Dread
Non notable writer

Patricia Driscoll (executive)
Non notable author: her only actual book was self-published by her foundation when she was president of it.

Lee DuCote
Non-notable writer, Salt and burn.

Naomi Duguid
not notable author

Richard Easter
Simply too marginal a writer.

John Edwards (Technology Writer)
Technology writer with no clear notability.

Jannion Steele Elliott
Self-published author of some non-notable books?

Mary Beth Ellis
Not a notable author.

Rifat Emin
Does not appear to be a notable poet/author.

R. M. Engelhardt
Unremarkable local poet from Albany, New York, USA.

Ari Enkin
Non-notable rabbi and author and blogger.

Herbie the Erbie
Author seems to be barely notable, via Google test

Edward M. Erdelac
Non-notable author/filmmaker.

Karl Bjorn Erickson
Utterly non-notable writer.

James Fahy
Non-notable author.

Daniel Falatko
Non-notable author.

Ryan Neil Falcone
Author of minor fiction that has been published in magazine.

Marie-Ange Faugérolas
Non-notable author.

Ngarto Februana
An author of question notability.

Alan Fenton
Non-notable author of non-notable fiction books.

Charity Gaye Finnestad
Non-notable author.

Jerome FitzGerald
Non-notable author.

Tom Fitzgerald
Non-notable author.

Tomas M Fleischmann
Self-published/paid-to-publish
author of questionable notability.

Will le Fleming
Author of a single book, which,
according to WorldCat, is found in
only 34 libraries.

Giovanna Fletcher
Non notable author.

Chris Flynn
Writer lacking notability, just a
man doing his job.

Nora Fountain
Non-notable author who self-
publishes via Amazon and
Smashwords.

Casey Fry
Completely non-notable writer.

Graeme Fuller
Non-notable author.

John G. Fuller
Seems like a non-notable author.

Jonathan Galland
Non-notable "health writer".

K. V. Gautam
Author of questionable notability.

Frank Gauthier
Apparently non-notable author, at
least one of whose works is self-
published.

Debora Geary
The subject appears to be the
author of several self published
books (Fireweed Publishing) but
shows no results in a Google News
search.

D Michelle Gent
Self-published author of
questionable notability.

Michael Gerber (parodist)
Non notable author.

Jane Gibian
Non-notable poet.

Edward Anthony Wharton Gill
Obscure early 20th century
academic and author.

Maurizio Giuliano
Non-notable author and UN official.

Yoel Glick
non notable author of self
published works.

Sheldon Goldfarb
Non-notable author.

Joel Goldman
Not a particularly notable author.

Slim Goodbuzz
Non notable anonymous author.

Henry Gould
Not notable poet blogger

Leopoldo Gout
Non-notable author.

Joshua Graham
Non notable writer.

Karen Graham (Dietitian)⌧
Being published does not
quite mean that that author is
neccesarially notable.

Stephen Grasso
Non notable, unpublished writer.

Case Greenfield
Does not appear to be a notable
author.

Emanuel Grigoras
Non-notable author.

Chander P. Grover
notability questionable/possible
author vanity/COI

Wayne Grudem
Not a notable author or theologian.

Peadar Ó Guilín
Non-notable author of one book...

Gujira
Un-notable author

Eileen P. Gunn
Writer, has published one book that
was mentioned in Newsday; does
not appear notable.

Gregory Wm. Gunn
Apparently non-notable author.

Shubham Gupta
The concerned writer has a minor
work of short stories.

Subodh Gupta (yoga trainer)
Non-notable author/trainer lacking
non-trivial support.

Rupert Haigh
Non-notable author of legal
training books for non-native
speakers of English.

Okano Hajime
Un-notable author

Andy Hamilton
Non notable author, not be
confused with comedian and writer
of the same name.

Kathryn Hamm
Nonnotable author.

Timo Hannay
Non-notable science writer/
publisher.

Bruno Hare
Subject appears to be a non-notable
author with only two recent books
and zero mentions in the Google
News archives.

William Hare
Non-notable author.

Matthew Joseph Harrington
Non-notable author: sole output
appears to be two short stories
in the shared-universe anthology
Man-Kzin Wars XI

Scott L. Harris
Non-notable pastor of local church,
former professor, and author.

Trudy Harris
Subject appears to be a barely
notable author of children's fiction.

Lisi Harrison
Unnotable author of a single series
of teen books.

Erin Hart
Non-notable author.

Harald K. Haugan
Non-notable author.

Keith hayes
Non notable author.

Rebecca Haynes
Being a (senior) university lecturer
and author of the odd published
work does not equate to notability.

Michael Henson
Non-notable author.

Christine Terhune Herrick
Unnotable author.

Clifford B. Hicks
Non-notable author.

Sander Hicks
Non-notable author/publisher.

Wayne Hoffman
Non-notable author.

Lucian Holland
He may be the son, grandson and
great-grandson of notable writers,
but is there any indication that he
himself is notable in any way?

Joe E. Holoubek
Non notable author.

Sanford Holst
a non-notable author whose books
appear to be self-published.

Brian Holtz
Unsucessful political candidate,
self-published author and blogger.

Wang Sheng Hong
Non-notable author lacking GHits
and GNEWS of substance.

Judith Hooper
Not notable beyond being the
author of one book.

Stephen Horne
Appears to be a non-notable writer.

Jason S. Hornsby
Author known for two books
published by vanity press
iUniverse.

Michael Horton
Non-notable author.

A.R. Horvath
Non-notable fiction writer.

Chris Howard
Non-notable writer who's published
a couple of non-notable short
stories and one non-notable book.

E.B. Hughes
Writer and film director of dubious
notability.

Hirbod Human
Writer/director of questionable
notability.

Jamie Humphreys
Not sufficently notable author.

Avalyn Hunter
Non-notable author of non-notable
books.

Wiesława Hunzvi
Non-notable Polish author.

Paula Huston
Seems to be a not-particularly-
notable author.

Chandra Kant Jaisansaria
Non-notable author.

Pete Jedick
Non-notable author lacking GHits
and GNEWS of substance to
support notability.

David John Jeffery
Author of unclear notability.

Edna Jeffrey
Non-notable businessperson and
author of a non-notable novel

Liam Jennings
Sefl-published author and book,
lacks notability

Christian Jensen (poet)
Non notable, unpublished writer.

Dizzle, Jim
Non-notable self-published author

Abby Johnson (activist)
Non-notable author of non-notable
book.

Michael Jones
Not a notable writer.

Shinozuka Jouji
Un-notable author

Derrick Judson
Author of one book to be printed in
2008 with no specified publisher?

Anatoly Borisovich Jurkin
Not notable author.

Carrie Kabak
Non-notable author.

Anil P. Kaveendra
Non-notable poet.

Sarah Kay
Unnotable young poet.

BML Hillen Keene
Non-notable author.

N.M. Kelby
Non-notable writer.

Raymond Kertezc
Kertezc is not a real person, but is a fake poet as part of a control question on a certain psychology test.

Oren Kessler
Non-notable writer lacking non-trivial support.

Sachin Ketkar
The subject is a non notable author.

Vinita Kinra
non notable author.

Selena Kitt
Non-notable author.

E.a. koetting
Author of questionable notability.

John Konrad
Konrad is described as an author, but his only book does not appear to have been commercially (or critically) successful.

M. Pat Korb
Non-notable therapist and author.

Donna Kossy
Non-notable book author.

Marton Kovacs
Apparently non notable author and advisor.

Jeff Koyen
Not a notable freelance writer and has no books either.

Anton Robert Krueger
Minor writer, did not win a major award or establish lasting contribution to field.

Myoma Myint Kywe
A Burmese author of questionable notability.

David Lagana
nn writer for WWE wrestling programs.

Kayla Ann Lambert
Nonnotable author.

Amy Lane
Non-notable writer who has paid notorious vanity-press iUniverse to print four non-notable books.

Connie Lapallo
Non notable author.

Jean Laroche
French poet, published a dozen books but it's not clear what their notability is.

Mark Lawrence
Non-notable author lacking ghits and gnews of substance.

Alan Lawson
Completely non-notable author.

Christopher Leadem
Non-notable author; all his works appear to have been self-published.

Anna Leahy
Non-notable writer.

Angela LeBlanc
Supposedly a published author, but a google search for her name didn't turn up with anything.

Adrien leduc
Self-published author with no indications of notability.

J. M. Lee
Being an author of a few sci-fi novels does not establish notability.

Ekram Ahmed Lelin
Non-notable poet.

Laura Lemay
Non-notable writer of computer books.

Sue Lenier
Poet who has garnered almost no media attention, yet is "superior to Shakespeare", "better than Ted Hughes", and "a much bigger thing than Sylvia Plath".

Jonell Lennon
Non-notable TV writer.

M G Leonard
As yet unpublished children's author.

Josh Levs
Non notable author.

Frontier Lift
Author does not establish notability.

Ryn Lilley
non-notable author.

Diane Lockward
Non-notable poet.

Bent Lorentzen
Not a notable Danish author.

Christopher Lotito
non-notable self-published author.

Jess Lourey
Non-notable author.

Ulli lust
Webcomic author of dubious notability.

Jon Lyndon
Non-notable author of self-published online poems and stories.

Bonnie Lyons
Non-notable writer and professor.

S. J. Maas
Non-notable author.

Marianne Macdonald
Unremarkable children's and
mystery author.

Will MacKinley
A self-published author (see
publisher details at amazon: and
the publisher's website who is
insufficiently notable)

Ghani Mahdi
Non-notable Algerian writer.

Mozid Mahmud
the poet has no notability.

Edward F. Malkowski
Non-notable author.

**William Morrison "The Bard of
Mallusk"**
Non-notable poet.

Virginia Marangell
Nonnotable author.

April Alisa Marquette
Non-notable author.

April Masini
Author of non-notable website and
books.

Darrin J Mason
Non-notable author whose one
novel to date was published by a
vanity publisher.

Peter D Matthews
Non-notable fringe author known
for having recently proposed
yet another hypothesis for the
Shakespeare authorship question.

Anna Jean Mayhew
non-notable writer.

Glenna Maynard
Unnotable author.

Eva McCall
Non-notable author.

Kevin McColley
Not notable as an author.

George McCoy
Non-notable author of a guide to
"massage parlours" (i.e. brothels) in
the UK.

Jenn McCreary
Non notable poet.

George Wallace Mcdonald
Author shows no inclination to
respond to the need to establish
notability.

Bella McFarland
Non-notable author lacking any
GNEWS and with no GHITS of
substance.

C. Matthew McMahon
Non-notable author/web designer.

Miles McMullan
Does not appear to be a notable author.

Suzanne McQueen
Non-notable entrepreneur and author.

Mease
Non-notable author of a book published by a vanity press.

Joseph William Bailey Hardman Medford
Non-notable author who's only book was on his family history.

Elizabeth Medina
Minor writer and translator.

Lynn Messina
Non-notable author.

Marissa Meyer
Unknown author, first book just released.

Mimori
Non-notable minor writer.

Gan Yao Ming
Non-notable author lacking GHits and GNEWS of substance.

Nabi Misdaq
Not a notable author.

Bibhuprasad Mohapatra
Non-notable author.

Carter Monroe
Apparently non-notable author.

Rima Morrell
May not meet the inclusion criteria for academics or authors.

Richard Moss
non-notable new age writer, referenced only to his own website.

Albert Mudrian
Non-notable author.

Gabriella Gutiérrez y Muhs
Dubious notability as an author.

Anupam Mukhopadhyay
Non-notable poet.

Martin Musatov
Non-notable screen writer.

Nazar Mohammad Mutmaeen
writer of unpublished books, appears to be non-notable anyway

Vihang Naik
Non notable poet.

Chandran Nair (entrepreneur)
author of one not very important book, which won an award from an online magazine of no particular authority.

Sarah Neumann
eBook author (possibly self-published) of questionable notability.

Jon K. Newton
non-notable author.

Janna Nickerson
Non-notable writer.

Louis van Niekerk
NN poet.

Robin P. Nolet
Non-notable author

Nick Noonan
Non-notable local author.

Barrie North
Non-notable author of technical
manuals.

Justin D. Nutt
Non-notable author.

Lise Nørgaard
Non-notable writer, no awards or
lasting impact of work.

Sean O'Connor
Non-notable writer/poet.

David Ohle
Non-notable writer lacking non-
trivial support.

Antony Oldknow
Non-notable writer.

Suzanne Marie Olsson
A self-published author who
believes Jesus is buried in Kashmir.

Chidi Anthony Opara
Apparently self-published internet
poet.

Bruno Osimo
Non-notable writer.

Jessica Pan
Non notable author.

Bhau Panchbhai
Non notable poet.

Ayushma Pandey
Non-notable writer.

Sharon Pearson
Not notable as an author.

Hayford Peirce
Non-notable author.

Dale Pendell
Non-notable fringe author and
poet.

Al Bermudez Pereira
Non-notable author lacking GHits
of substance and with no GNEWS.

Janet, Perkins
NN, self-published author, host of
local, self-produced CATV show

Freddie Lee Peterkin
Non-notable musician and author.

Barry Peters
Unremarkable author and teacher.

David Peterson
Internet writer with no indication
of notability.

Vanessa Van Petten
Author with one self-published
book (the publisher iUniverse
describes itself as "Self Publishing
Company").

Edward Pinkowski
Appear to be non-notable writer.

Alan Pipes
non notable writer, mentioned once
in Daily Telegraph for collecting
unusual cycle lanes, web master of
a channel 4 tv programme's website
and managing editor of a CAD
magazine in the last 70' s...

William Pitcock
Non notable software author.

Soth Polin
Non-notable Cambodian writer.

Rolf Potts
Minor writer.

Thomm Quackenbush
Unremarkable e-book author.

Justin Quarry
Non-notable writer.

Maura Quint
NN notable writer.

Praveen Crypty R
Non-notable author.

Pankaj Rag
Non Notable author and mid level
civil servant

Roger Rawlings
Non-notable author.

Michelle Reale
Not notable either as a poet or a
librarian.

Raphaël Reclus
Possibly non-notable author.

Skyler Reep
Non-notable self-improvement
author.

Suzanna Reeves
Non-notable author/singer lacking
non-trivial support.

Christian Rehm
Clearly not a notable author or
politician.

Factions: Revenge of the Reich
No mention after a google search of
title, only a few in passing mention
of author.

Stewart Reuben
A mere chess organizer and author
of some books on poker nobody
bought.

Marilyn Reynolds
Non-notable author.

D.C. Rhind
Non-notable author.

Robert T. Rhode
Non-notable author.

Dan Richardson
Non-notable author.

Jason Rider
Apparently non-notable author whose books are published through vanity press PublishAmerica.

Chris Riseley
Non-notable comic author.

Ahsaan Rizvi
Not a notable author.

Katharine "Kat" Bear-Diemer Robinson
Very minor author and tv-producer.

KEVIN ROLLE
Only ghits for Kevin D. Rolle is a comedy/comic strip writer; unverifiable, non-notable.

Nick Rosen
Non-notable author.

Meryl Runion
Non-notable author lacking GHits and GNEWS of substance.

Marie Rutkoski
Non notable author

Carrie Ryan
Non-notable author whose first book has yet to be published.

Matthew J. Sadler
Non-notable poet.

Jostein Saether
Not notable, obscure writer.

Kunwar Mohinder Singh Bedi Sahar
Non-notable poet.

Mayu Sakai
Unnotable manga author.

Jim Salmon
Non-notable author.

Leslie Lee Sanders
Apparently non-notable author who has published three books through vanity press.

Greg M. Sarwa
Non-notable author.

Willis Schalliol
He's a vet and an author, but apparently a non-notable one.

Terry D. Scheerer
Science-fiction writer of doubtful notability.

Don Schlesinger
Author of a single gaming book and website.

Michael Segedy
Non-notable writer.

Arunabha Sengupta
Non notable author.

Ahmad Shafaat
The author appears to be neither notable as a mathematician nor as an Islamic scholar.

Hafiz Muhammad Shariq
Non-notable author.

Aiden Shaw
Apparently non-notable author/ model.

Durk Simmons
Non-notable writer whose only book was published by vanity press AuthorHouse.

Harold L. Sirkin
Non-notable consultant and author.

Robert Morning Sky
Non-notable UFOlogist and author.

Angela Slatter
Non-notable author lacking GHits and GNEWS of substance.

Miriam Slozberg
Non notable author - - the books have no library holdings at all in Worldcat and appear to be self published.

Robert F. Smallwood
Writer whose books are all out from notorious vanity press BookSurge.

Ashley Smith (journalist)
Non-notable writer and political organizer.

Jessica Smith
Nonnotable young selfpublished poet.

Adam M. Snow
Non-notable poet.

Raji Sohal
Unremarkable freelance writer/ stylist.

Andrew Spear
Non notable author of 3 non-notable books, in the adjacent nominations.

Jane Speed
Non-notable radio writer.

Anna Joy Springer
Non notable author; A/c worldcat, her first book is in only 13 libraries, her second in only 2.

Meaburn Staniland
unimportant author.

Rudolph Frederick Stapelberg
Non-notable author of technical books.

R.H. Stavis
Non-notable author.

Graziano Stefanelli
Non-notable author of one novel.

Aron Steinke
Self-published author.

Darren Stephens
Non-notable self published author lacking GHITS and GHITS of substance.

Sam Stephenson
Sam Stephenson seems to be a minor writer.

Benjamin Sternick
An "author" who has not been published.

Samantha Stewart
Un-notable author.

Edo Stojčić
A minor journalist and writer.

Brett Edward Stout
Non-notable author, his work is self-published.

Paul M. Strickler
Non-notable author.

Kenneth Arthur Stroud
Non-notable author.

Øyvind Strømmen
The author is not himself notable.

Clifford Allan Sullivan
Self published author/independent filmmaker of questionable notability.

Mark I. Sutherland
Sutherland is, to be sure, a published author, but there is no indication that he is notable as an author.

Mark Sutherland
Non-notable author lacking non-trivial support.

Haryono Suyono
Non notable speech writer, website no longer exists

Julia Suzuki
Apparently non-notable author.

Hannibal Tabu
Non-notable writer.

Clay Tarver
Not notable as a guitarist or writer.

Manuel Romero Mier y Terán
Non-notable author (less than 10 hits on Google search)

Dick Teresi
Non-notable author; attempting
to piggyback on the fact that he
ghostwrote or co-wrote a book
with a notable scientist.

Edward Payson Terhune
Unnotable pastor and author.

Meg Thomann
A writer, editor not in any news.

David N. Thomas
Non-notable author of non-notable
books.

Duerre thomas
Nonnotable author/preacher,
appears to be self-promotional.

Caroline H Thompson
Non-notable fringe science author.

Nathan Thoms
Author with one self-published
book based on own thesis.

Jonty Tiplady
Non-notable poet.

Paul Tomkins
There's no debating he's a writer,
but he is simply not notable.

EJ Topping
Non-notable author lacking GHits
and GNEWS of substance.

Troy Townsin
Non-notable author of non-notable
books.

Rosemary Winters Tracey
Poet, with one self published work
in amazon, & nothing on worldcat.

Jack travers
Non-notable teacher and author.

William S. Tribell
Non-notable up-and-coming minor
poet.

Michael Trice
NN author.

Lynne Triplett
Non-notable comic book author
lacking ghits and Gnews of
substance.

Lars R. Trodson
Non notable author.

Seth Tucker
Non-notable author.

Joe Turman
Non-notable author with zero
GNEWS and no GHits of substance
to support notability.

Susan Tuttle
Non-notable teacher and writer.

Harilal Upadhyay
Seemingly NN author.

Akinobu Uraka
Non-notable author known for only one work.

Ardashir Vakil
Low notability author.

Mike Vance
A supposed poet whose existence is unverifiable.

Thomas L. Vaultonburg
Self-published writer of questionable notability.

Lee Vayle
Not a notable author in that he wrote a hagiography of William M. Branham.

Kyle Veazey
Doesn't seem to be a notable writer.

Kelly Velayas
Non-notable author.

Anthony Venn-Brown
Non-notable author.

Pablo Villaça
Non-notable writer.

Sri Vishwanath
Non-notable author lacking ghits and Gnews.

Adrian Volts
Non-notable author of seemingly non-published work.

Norb Vonnegut
Non-notable blogger and author of a single novel.

Traeonna Wagener
Non-notable occult author, only one minor book published.

Hilary Wagner
Non-notable author.

Lars Walker
There's no indication that Walker meets the standards of notability for authors.

David Walks-As-Bear
Non-notable author.

Shanxing Wang
Another non-notable poet.

Dustin Warburton
Apparent self-published author of questionable notability.

Iris Wedgwood
Non-notable writer who apparently was part of the British aristocracy.

Clara Louisa Wells
Non-notable author.

Robison Wells
Mormon author with some books published on a tiny Mormon-only press, so tiny that Amazon.com and other booksellers do not carry any of its titles.

Celeste West
nON-NOTABLE author.

Krista White (matchmaker)
Appears to fail to meet the
notability criteria for authors.

Lowell Mick White
Non-notable author lacking GHits
and GNEWS of substance.

Michael Whiteacre
Non-notable producer, writer,
filmmaker, distributor, etc.

Lee Whitnum
Non-notable, self-published author
running for Senate.

Robert Wickman
Non notable writer.

David Wilcock
Spiritualism author with a best-
selling book but no real mention
outside the field.

Jason D. Wilkins
Non-notable poet.

Greg Wilkovich
Non notable author and poet.

Connie Williams
non notable author.

Darren wills
Non-notable "author".

Wayne Loren Wilson
Non notable author.

Douglas E. Winter
non notable writer and lawyer.

Ashley A. Wood
Comic book writer of questionable
notability.

William A. Woodall
Author doesn't appear to be
notable.

Sean woodward
As a writer, he seems to have
limited and only local notability.

Thomas E. Woodward
Author of two books promoting
pseudoscience (creationism).

Larry Woody
Non-notable writer.

Eileen Workman
Writer with 1 book, published by
almost unknown publisher.

Michael Orlando Yaccarino
Non-notable author.

Sima Yari
Nonnotable selfpublished poet.

Shmuel Yerushalmi
NN unpublished "protest poet",
casually mentioned in one news
story.

Alexa Young
Unnotable author.

Rob Young
NN writer/editor.

Brigit Kelly Young
Non-notable writer lacking GHits
and GNEWS of substance.

Walter S. Zapotoczny Jr.
Self-published author: his 2009 noel
is in two libraries only according to
worldcat; the other two books are
not in worldcat at all.

Adam Zelga
Non-notable author.

Gary Zenker
Not a notable author

Stephen Zhang
Apparently non-notable author.

Darko Žlebnik
A non-notable writer from
Slovenia.

Benjamin Žnidaršič
A non-notable poet and artist.

Cartoonist

Grant Bond
Minor and non-notable comic book
artist.

Charlie Darenne
French cartoonist completly
unknown, even in France

Baron Barrymore Halpenny
Artist/cartoonist of questionable
notability.

Mike Pearse
Non-notable cartoonist.

David Willis
Non-notable web comic artist

Cinematographer

Anupap Buachand
Cinematographer who has only
worked on 2 films.

Paul Deng
Non-notable cinematographer.

Alex Gilbert
Non-notable cinematographer.

Yuri Pirondi
Non-notable photographer,
videographer and cinematographer.

Ioana Vasile
Not a single one of the films for
which she has been credited as
DP or cinematographer has been
widely reviewed (let alone has
had a review comment on the
cinematography).

Dancer

Kelli Baker
Non-notable dancer, only played minor roles in the High School Musical series.

Rachel Howe
Non-notable dancer.

Zin kyaw kyaw
Non-notable dancer/university student.

Yana Lewis
A dancer/choreographer of unknown/unreferenced notability

Kashif Memon
Non-notable dancer who auditioned for America's Got Talent.

Charonne Mose
Non-notable dancer with only lead of notability being a 1995 Emmy winning for Miss America with several Books results showing.

Danielle Peazer
Not notable dancer.

Alexis Villegas
Non-notable backup dancer/actor lacking GHits and GNEWS of susbstance.

Fashion designer

Janet Howard
Fashion designer but it's not clear
she is notable.

Rina Palma
vanity, freshly graduated fashion
designer`'

Film director

Bryan Binder
Film director of questionable notability.

Tyler Funk
Film director of questionable notability.

John Luther Schofill, Jr.
Interesting but apparently non-person, film director and academic, lover of classical music.

Illustrator

Steve Adams
NN illustrator.

Shinod Akkaraparambil
Non-notable artist / illustrator.

Malou Bonicos
Non-notable illustrator who created an obscure children's series.

Janet Hamlin
She is a technical illustrator who got a complain because she drew someones nose too big.

A.J. Hateley
British illustrator who has some fame in the blogosphere but hasn't been the subject of any in-depth media attention.

Kazuyuki Kurashima
Japanese illustrator with a handful of video game credits, but he isn't even the main artist/art director on most of those games.

Mato
Illustrator known mainly for Pokemon Adventures manga but nothing else.

Sara Rapoport
Non-notable illustrator.

Zina Saunders
non notable writer and illustrator, with no major works or awards.

Sarah M. Tillman
Non-notable illustrator.

Martial artist

Isagani Abon
Non-notable martial artist

Carlos Aveline
Non-notable martial artist

Robert Brutus Beal
Non notable martial artist.

Marc-Andre Bergeron (taekwondo)
Non-notable martial artist.

Gerard Blaize
Non notable martial artist.

Micah Brock
Non-notable as martial artist or youtube persona.

Otto Cardew
Non notable martial artist/Martial Arts instructor.

George Cofield
Non notable martial artist.

Aaron Cohen (judoka)
Irrelevant martial artist.

Bernard Collins
Non-notable martial artist.

Alberto Crane
Non-notable MMA fighter or martial artist.

Anthony DeFalco
Subject fails to meet the notability requirements for either indoor football players or martial artists.

Keyvan Dehnad
Non-notable martial artist.

Alexis Dufresne
Competing as a BJJ blue belt does not meet the notability criteria for martial artists or athletes.

Todd Dunphy
Non-notable martial artist.

Ahmed Ennaji
Not notable as either scientist or martial artist.

Michael G. Foster
Non-notable martial artist.

Michelle Gordon
Non-notable martial artist.

Cesar Gracie
Non-notable martial artist.

Crosley Gracie
Non-notable as martial artist or MMA fighter.

Steve Grody
No indication of notability as a martial artist or "graffiti documentarian".

Abdelwahid Habibullah
Non-notable martial artists.

Petar Jevremovic
Non-notable martial artist.

Michael hairston jr
Non-notable martial artist.

Kim Kahana
Doesn't seem to meet any notability criteria since he doesn't appear notable as an entertainer, military man, or martial artist.

Ik Jo Kang
Non-notable martial artist with a dojo.

Ryan Kilmartin
Non notable basketball player and martial artist.

Den Klyuev
Non-notable martial artist.

Jack Krystek
Non-notable martial artist.

Ronald Gan Ledesma
Non-notable as either a martial artists or director.

Terry Lim
Non-notable martial artist lacking non-trivial support.

Pavel Los
Non-notable martial artist.

Robert Lovi
Non notable martial artist.

Renato Magno
Non-notable martial artist.

Neil Owen McEvoy
Non-notable martial artist.

Raymond Mkhize
Non-notable martial artist.

Damian Mohler
Non notable martial artist.

Paul Mormando
Non-notable martial artist (self awarded high rank).

Avi Moyal
Non-notable martial artist.

Greg Nelson
Non-notable martial artist.

Felipe "Zicró" Neto
Non-notable martial artist

Johnny Tri Nguyen
Lacks notability as either a martial artist or stuntman.

Joe Palanzo
A non notable martial artist who is just as unnotable as Worldwide Kenpo Karate Association the organisation founded by him.

Jerry Piddington
Non-notable martial artist.

Marif Piraev
Non-notable mixed martial artist.

Richard Rabago
Appears to be a non-notable
martial artist.

Robey Reed
There's no indication that he meets
any of the notability criteria for
martial artists.

Diane Reeve
Non-notable martial artist - owner
of a single school.

Vernon Rieta
There's nothing to show he meets
the notability standards for martial
artists.

Michel van Rijt
Non-notable martial artist.

Massimo Rizzoli
Non-notable martial artist.

Pradipta Kumar Roy
Non-notable martial artist.

Frank E. Sanchez
Non-notable martial artist.

Olaf Simon
Not notable martial artist.

Ernest R. Smith
Non-notable martial artist.

Harold Rogelio Laranang Sr.
Non-notable martial artist.

Joaquim Valente
Non-notable martial artist.

Fredrick J. Villari
Non notable martial artist.

Jon Wiedenman
Non-notable martial artist.

Jay T. Will
Non-notable martial artist.

David Wilson
Non-notable martial artist.

Kristian Woodmansee
Non-notable martial artists - all
competitions were under belt.

Hataya Mitsuo Yoshitoki
Non-notable martial artist.

Kendall Yount
Not yet notable as a martial artist
because all of her titles are as a
junior.

Model

Rosil Al Azawi
Appears to be a non-notable fashion model.

Sigrid Åhs
Non-notable model.

Amanda Babin
Non-Notable Model who appeared on America's Next Top Model.

Warren Baker
Non-notable model/actor lacking GHits and GNEWS of substance.

Catriona Balfe
Non-notable fashion model.

Sondra Barker
Non-notable model.

Arlene Baxter
Non-notable model.

Lucy Becker
non-notable model.

Lhea Bernardino
Non-notable model.

Gigi St. Blaque
Non-notable short-term glamour model with one minor film role.

Trisha Campbell
Non-notable adult model.

Heather Carolin
Non-notable model.

Kelly Carrington
Not notable model who played volleyball at high school.

Nina Carter
non notable former model

Analicia Chaves
A model.

Selina Chippy
Model and runner-up in a minor beauty pageant.

Jenny Chu
Non-notable car show model.

Kim Cloutier
Non notable model.

Sam Cooke
non notable former model

Andrew Cooper
Non-notable model lacking non-trivial, secondary support.

Deborah Corrigan
non notable former model

Mariana Bridi da Costa
No notability except gruesome death and fact that she was a model.

Chelsea darling
Non-notable model.

Natalie Denning
non notable former model

Katerena DePasquale
Non-notable model / clothing
designer.

Regina Deutinger
Non-notable model.

Asia DeVinyl
Non Notable model.

Katarzyna Dolinska
Subject fails both general notability
requirements and notability
requirements for models.

Jessica Dykstra
Non-notable model lackng GHits
and Gnews of substance.

Rachel Echelberger
An aspiring model who was
eliminated on episode 3 of the
thirteenth season of America's Next
Top Model.

Lacey Von Erich
not notable yet professional
wrestler & model

Malene Espensen
non notable former model

Kimberly Evenson
Porn starNude model (correction)
that fails to meet criteria.

Dors Feline
Non-notable nude model.

Kathy Ferreiro
Non notable model who is only
known for being a look alike

Barbara Fialho
Non-notable model.

Kimberly Fisher
Non-notable model.

Autumn Le Fleur
Non-notable businesswoman and
bondage model.

Mary Forsberg
Marrying someone notable,
working as a model, and having
had a bit part in a barely notable
film does not equate to notability.

Lianna Fowler
Only her notability in Britain's Next
Top Model and failing orphaned.

Alice Goodwin
nN model.

Amy Green
non notable former model

Kelly Hall
non notable former model

Raven Hanson
Non-notable model.

Siobhan Harrell
Non-notable model.

Jessica hatch
Non notable model.

Alexa Heart
nn "interactive adult show" model.

DJ Heavygrinder
Non-notable model and DJ.

Ruth Higham
non notable former model

Mark Hobart
Non-notable model/actor.

Vicki Hodge
non notable former model

Roxanne K. Hyunah
Non notable model.

Melanie Jane
non notable former model

Tracy Kirby
non notable former model

Arthur Kulkov
Non-notable model lacking Ghtis and GNEWS of substance.

Akira Lane
Non-notable pornographic model.

Shakyra LaShae
Unremarkable model/actress.

Damaris Lewis
Non notable model.

Amanda Lexx
Glamour model with brief porn career whose most significant achievement appears to be a single picture in Playboy.

Katie Lisel
Non-notable teen model.

Rina Lorilla
Non-notable model/no notability asserted.

Linda Lusardi
non notable former model

Tiffany Lynn
An model/actress, who appears to be not notable.

Jasmine Mai
Non-notable adult model.

Marilinda
Only notable for being the winning model of Project Runway 3.

Michelle Marsh
non notable former model

Lilit Martirosyan
Model who won a preliminarily round to minor event - Top Model of the World.

Elena Melnik
Run-of-the-mill model.

Daniel Miagany
Nonnotable male fashion model

Suzanne Mizzi
non notable former model

Alexandra Moore
Being an Internet nude/glamour model with big tits is not notable.

Daniella Morris
Daniella Morris (born July 25, 1989) appears to be a non-notable teen pageant model.

Isley nicole
According to her IMDB credits her roles mainly consist of names along the lines of: Beautiful Babe, Maid, Fantasy Girl, Friend, and repeatedly being Trophy Model for BET.

Sandra Nilsson
Non-notable model.

Robert Niter
A recent winner of championship, a model, a bodybuilder who is not in the news.

L'Wren Nycole
Not notable fashion model.

Diana O'Brien
Does not seem to have been notable as a model, or for any other reason, prior to her death.

Kay O'Hara
Modern pin-up model.

Princess kelechi oghene
Non-notable model, "socialite", and "ambassador" for a drug manufacturer.

Taya Parker
Non-notable model had some non-outstanding jobs.

Natasha Pestano
non notable model/actress.

Dominique Piek
Non notable model.

Tori Praver
Non notable model.

Naomi Preizler
Minor model - mostly just a couple seasons of runway work.

Sophie Price
Apparently one-time glamour model whose primary clame to fame is being the sister of Katie Price, but notability is not inherited.

Dagus and Rockwood Railroad
Appears to be an entirely non-notable model railroad.

Sonali Raut
A model/actress that basically falls under too soon.

Maripily Rivera
Non-notable model from Puerto Rico, best known for being married

to baseball star Roberto Alomar.

Michele Rogers
Non-notable model.

Anka Romensky
Non-notable model.

Milena Leticia Roucka
nn model/independent wrestling manager.

Dean Rowland
Non-notable, apparently a former fashion model now hoping to establish a blog.

Adam Sabbagh
Non-notable model.

Garry Sahota
Non-notable model with a few minor roles in music videos and supporting roles in a few films.

Laura Scaife
Second place getter in the reality program New Zealand's Next Top Model.

Eric Ahlqvist Scott
Co-founder of a non-notable company and model of no apparent notability.

Sarah Seewar
Non notable model.

Maria Sheriff
non notable former model

Charmaine Sinclair
non notable former model

Ananya Soni
Non-notable model.

Elvira Stehr
A finalist in Philippines' Next Top Model hasn't won and does not meet notability requirements.

Eboni Stocks
only notable for her involvement in Australia's Next Top Model.

Skye Stracke
Non-notable model.

Lindsey Strutt
non notable former model

Cassie Sumner
non notable former model

Peta Todd
non notable former model

Aimi Tomori
Some random Japanese model.

Abigail Toyne
Non-notable erotic model.

Ashley Ann Vickers
Another model trying to be notable.

Hana Vitvarova
A fairly nonnotable Czech adult model.

Annemarie vola
non-notable model.

Sarah Vonderhaar
Eliminated contestant on Top
Model, and currently at a career
crossroads.

Jennifer Walcott
Non-notable model has done a lot
of minor works.

Madison Welch
non notable former model

Giulliana Weston
Non-notable model.

Kate Winton
Non-notable glamour model

Musician

Anish 1
Non-notable musician.

Ginger 102
A google search on the band and lead singer reveals only the myspace account.

Kristoff Abrenica
Non-notable musician.

Acidburp
Non-notable musician

Giovanni Adamo
Not notable musician

JME Adenuga
Non-notable musician.

Adriiana
Non-notable singer.

Assaf Adry
Non-notable musician.

Mahdyar Aghajani
Non-notable musician.

AJ (South Korean singer)
Non-notable singer.

Ife Akintayo
Non-notable "singer/actress".

Bryan alan
Non-notable musician.

Aaron J. Albano
Singer/actor lacking significant credits and notice.

Razvan albu
Non-notable musician by an SPA.

Nichole Alden
Non-notable musician.

Mary Alessi
non notable christian contemporary musician.

Aliya (singer)
Unsigned, never-signed artist

Tiffany Jo Allen
Non-notable singer, she has never been signed to a major label or had any chart singles on major music charts.

The AllStars
Non-notable group of session musicians.

Zayra Alvarez
Non-notable musician.

Generous alzir!
Musician with some playtime, but most ghits are Myspace/etc.

Siriporn Ampaipong
Non-notable singer.

Robert 'Skins' Anderson
Non-notable musician.

Aneel
Musician of questionable notability.

Stephanie Angelini
Non-notable singer.

Lauren Aquilina
Non-notable musician.

Arcangel
Non-notable reggaeton artist.

Roger Argenis
Two non-notable singers.

Arielle (singer)
Singer may not meet music
notability requirements.

Arlyn
Non-notable musician who has yet
to release a debut album.

Katie Armiger
Yet another "up-and-coming" non-
notable singer.

Riley Armstrong
non notable christian rock singer.

Atllas
Musician with two albums, released
only on his own label.

Kristian Attard
Non-notable musician.

Auburn
Non-notable singer signed to a
non-notable record label who has
yet to release a single or album.

Landon Austin
Non-notable musician.

B-Valentine
Musician of questionable notability.

B.rite
Non Notable Musician, artist and
related albums have nearly zero
ghits, lack of mentions in any sort
of publication.

Greg Bacon
Appears to be a non-notable
musician.

Richard Bailey (drummer)
Non-notable session musician.

Pfuri Baldenweg
Non-notable musician.

Dave Ball
Non-notable musician.

Veronica Ballestrini
Doesn't seem to be a notable singer.

Jacob Bannon
Singer for non-notable (or at best,
marginally notable) band.

Shlomi Bar'el
Non-notable singer.

Brittany Barber
Non-notable musician, only self-released material.

Darren Bartlett
A Google News Archive search for ["Darren Bartlett" composer | singer | pianist | piano | vocalist | vocals] provided me with just two unimpressive hits.

Loshaarn Bastian
Non-notable musician.

Aza Bataeva
Fails notability criteria for musicians.

Bucky Baxter
Obscure sessions musician and Dylan sideman; like many sessions musicians, undoubtedly a consummate pro, but not notable.

Chris Beale
Non-notable musician.

Beast1333
Non-notable musician.

Dean De Benedictis
Non-notable minor musician.

Ola Bergman
A musician with no info really.

Rick Berlin
Non-notable local musician.

JS aka The Best
Non-notable musician.

Justin Bibis
A duo of VERY young singers who are basically under too soon.

Scotty bills
Non-notable lead singer of a non-notable band.

Bonnie Bishop
Potentially non-notable country singer.

Boac (rapper)
Non notable artists.

Jimmy Bondoc
NN musician.

Angel Bouchet
Non-notable musician.

Magic Box
Non-notable singer.

Coste Boy (El General)
Non-notable musician.

Owen Brady
Non-notable Irish jazz musician who has just released his first album.

Bartosz Brenes
Non-notable musician.

Kenneth Brian
American musician.

Charls Brown
Non-notable musician.

Stacee Brown
Non-notable singer.

Chuck Brown (New Age musician)
Does not appear to be a notable musician.

Judy Brown
A B-movie bit player, a minor jeweller and an unsuccessful singer?

Dalal Bruchmann
Non notable musician.

Brian Brushwood
Non-notable stage musician claiming fame for having obscure shows on two microscopic "podcast networks" that barely meet notability standards themselves, and for having been on the Tonight Show once.

Bubba-T
Does not meet notability requirements for musicians.

Sean De Burca
Non-notable musician.

Malena Burke
Non-Notable Cuban singer.

Ed Butcher
Non-notable musician.

Jonathan Byrd
Non-notable musician.

Kasi calvin
Non-notable musician.

Violet The Cannibal
Non-notable musician.

Jenks "Tex" Carman
Non notable musician.

John Carroll
Not a notable musician.

John Carta
Non-notable musician.

Jonathan Casey
Non-notable musician.

Leigh Casino
Appears to be a non-notable musician; all google hits on "Leigh Casino" seem to be turning up other notices.

Nolyn Casino
Unremarkable hip-hop artist.

FAME CERTIFIED
Non-notable musician.

Mosotho chakela
Singer whose album and record company cannot be found on Google.

Eric Chamberlain
Non-notable musician and graphic artist.

Charmaine
Non notable singer.

Loren Chasse
fails musician notability criteria

Chemda
Non-notable podcast host and musician.

Gorilla Chilla
Open and shut case of non-significant small scale musician.

Valentine Chin
Non-notable session musician.

Oz Chiri
Non-notable musician

Jonas Raskolnikov Christiansen
Non-notable musician.

Gianni Cicogna
Non-notable musician.

Jay D Clark
Non notable musician.

David Clement
Non-notable musician.

Michael Cleveland (bluegrass musician)
Possibly the artist doesn't meet notability for a musician.

Ollie Cole
Apparently non-notable musician, who was a member of band which briefly had minor success.

Compa
Non-notable musician.

Dan Connolly
Dubious notability musician.

Ross copperman
Non-notable musician.

Hona Costello
No sign of notability: unsigned artist, who only self-released 1 EP via the internet.

Clayton Counts
Musician whose sole accomplishment seems to be getting a cease and desist from record labels for releasing a mashup album Sgt. Petsound's Lonely Hearts Club Band on his blog.

Jon Courtney
Singer/songwriter in middlingly-notable alternative band.

Criizter
Unnotable musician.

Crystin
unremarkable singer/musician?

Alberto Ctllo
Non-notable musician.

Larry Cutrone
Non-notable " American Musician/
Comedian/Writer.

Winky D
Non notable musician whose sole
achievement seems to have been to
win a sort of battle of the bands in
Zimbabwe.

D-Pryde (rapper)
Non-notable musician...

D-Stroy
Non notable musician

Ben Daglish
Non-notable musician.

Mick Dalla-Vee
Non-notable musician.

Jack Dalrymple
Individually non-notable musician.

Paddy Dalton (Songwriter)
Non-notable musician.

Paul Stuart Davies
Non-notable musician.

Brad Davis
Played with a few notable
musicians but that doesn't make
him notable himself.

Dominic davis
Non-notable musician.

Andrea Dätwyler
Singer in a notable band, but isn't
notable in her own right.

Mayestron Deba
Potentially non-notable musician.

Pia December
non notable singer songwriter, head
of non notable music publisher

Krazy Dee
Non-notable musician/rapper.

Kelly Denis
Non notable self promoted
musician.

Mihaela Dinu
Singer is non-notable.

Diane DiPiazza
Not notable former musician.

Boma Diri
Non-notable singer lacking ghits
and Gnews of substance.

Dutch Dirty
Non-notable musician.

El DoboLocoPapo
Non notable myspace music artist

Maxi Dolan
Non-notable musician.

DJ Doughboy
Non-notable musician.

Patrick Doval
Non-notable musician.

George Dragon
Does not meet the notability requirements for a writer or musician.

Driftbomb
Non-notable musician lacking non-trivial support.

Dubbledge
Non-notable musician; has released 1 album, 1 mixtape—no hit singles.

Young Duece
non notable musicians.

Ariana Dvornik
Non-notable singer/actress.

E-Dawg
Non Notable musician.

E.Stonji
Musician with no notability at all.

Cud Eastbound
Non-notable musician.

Mark Edwards (harpsichordist)
Non-notable musician.

Mary Edwards
Not notable musician.

Aksyn Elek
Non-notable musician.

Patrick Elkins
Non-notable musician and puppeteer.

Jade Ell
Non-notable musician.

Bastian Emig
Non-notable musician.

Jude Enemy
Potentially non-notable musician.

Karl Engelmann
Non-notable musician.

Andrei Eremin
Notability is not inherited and he's only mentioned in connection with musicians he worked with.

Erene
Singer does not appear to be notable.

Conchita Espinosa
Non-notable musician.

Jake Evans
Non-notable musician.

Princess Eze
Non-notable musician.

Tito Falaschi
Unnotable musician.

Fannius III
Non-notable singer.

Francesco Fareri
Non-notable musician.

Shadab Faridi
Non notable musician.

Fash
Non-notable musician.

Regin Le Faye
Non-notable singer/songwriter.

Schuyler Feigen
Unremarkable musician.

Evan Feldman
borderline musician.

Marcelo Feldman
Non-notable musician.

Little fire
Non-notable musician.

Dirt Fishermen
Nonnotable musicians in a
nonnotable band.

Nikki Flores
Non-notable singer.

Flow
Non-notable singer.

Limuel B. Forgey III
Subject has not had a significant
or notable career as a professional
opera singer.

Mazaradi Fox (rapper)
Non-notable artist; signed to a label
but has not released an album.

Iain Frampton
Non-notable musician.

Beverly Fre$h
Non notable musician.

Micki Free
nn musician

Kill Freeman
non notable musician.

Mike Fury
Does not seem to be notable either
as a journalist or as a musician.

Mord Fustang
Musician of dubious notability.

Gaise
Not notable musician who fails the
notability criteria.

John Galea (singer/songwriter)
Non-notable musician.

Andy J Gallagher
Non-notable musician.

Jimmy Gallagher (sax)
Non-notable musician.

Chris Garver
Singer / songwriter, music entirely
self-released or released on
"Pilcrow Records".

Matt Gauss
Non-notable musician.

Ghetto (rapper)
non-notable artist

Parul Ghosh
Non-Notable singer.

Gilanyan
Musician with no apparent real
assertion of notability.

Brianna Gilmore
Non-notable musician.

The Paradiso Girls
Non-notable band of non-notable
"singers" with no records, just hype
(and that feeble)

Bobby Goldfingers
Non-notable singer belonging to a
non-notable band.

Dave Gonzalez
Doesn't seem to be a notable
musician.

Matt Good (American musician)
Non-notable musician.

Tim Gordon
Singer lacking notability.

Jeremy W. Goss
Non-notable musician.

Chad Gould
does not seem to be notable enough
either as a footballer or a musician

Amanda Grace
Non-notable musician.

Andy Grammer
non notable unsigned singer

Gina Green
Non-notable gospel singer

Grant Green, Jr.
Non-notable musician.

Jeff Gretz
Non-notable musician.

Eddie Grey (Composer)
Non-notable musician.

Bruno Grife
Non-notable musician.

Chelcee Grimes
Singer/songwriter signed to a label
but with no releases.

Larkin Grimm
Non-notable musician.

DJ Grind
Non-notable musician; radio host,
mixtapes and YouTube, nothing
noteworthy.

Grynch
Non notable hip hop artist.

Carmine Guida
Fails notability requirements for musicians.

'The Joe' Gurba
Non-notable musician lacking GHits and GNEWS of substance.

Peter Gutteridge
NN musician.

Karol Gwóźdź
nn musician

H-Eugene
Non-notable musician.

Hossein Hadisi
Non notable musician.

Simya hamdan
Non-notable singer.

Steve Hamilton
Does not appear to a very notable musician

Michael Hamnett
Non-notable musician and academic (?).

Larry Hansen
Artist is not notable, nor is the band.

Latoya Hanson
Singer who is unnotable without her group.

Steve Hardin
Subject fails to meet notability requirements for musicians and songwriters

Amina Harris
Non-notable artist, only had one semi-hit feature single so far (which doesn't even qualify as a "hit," as it only peaked at #41).

Jane Harvey
Non-notable editor and musician.

Mekaal Hasan
Non-notable musician.

Cyril Havermans
Non-notable musician.

Calvin Hayes
Non-notable musician

Frankie Hayze
Non-notable musician.

Fenno Heath
Musician lacking notability.

Kalyn Heffernan
Non notable musician.

Joshua Helgason
Non-notable musician.

Xuan Pablo Hergon
Non-notable singer/actor lacking GNEWS and GHits of substance.

Mikkel Hess
Non-notable musician.

Chel Hill
Non-notable musician.

Mission Hill (band)
Doesn't appear to meet any of the
the notability criteria for musicians
and ensembles.

Vanessa Hillman
Non-notable local singer.

Olivia Hime
Non-notable singer and lyricist.

Mark Hinch
Nonnotable musician.

Fatal Hitchkoch
Not a notable musician.

Pea Hix
Non-notable musician.

Josh Hoge
Non-notable musician.

Ryan Thomas Holley
Non-notable musician who is part
of a non-notable band.

Holmes Ives
Non-notable musician.

Vahco Before Horses
Non notable musician.

Stefan Hruscă
not notable seasonal Hungarian
folk singer

Ivan Hrvatska
Singer with very little notability;
ghits point mainly to blogs/
MySpace/social networking sites.

Matt Hubbard
Non-notable musician lacking
GHits and GNEWS of substance.

Mark Hunstone
Seemingly non-notable musician.

Shannon Hurley
Non-notable musician/singer-
songwriter.

Nipsey Hussle
Non-notable musician with only
mixtapes to his credit.

Shuja Hyder
Non-notable singer.

Hypasounds
Barbadian soca artist with no
albums, previous nominee for
Barbados Music Award.

Lee Ji Hyun
Non notable singer.

MC Funky J
Non notable musician.

Flap jack
Non-notable musician.

Wyatt Jackson
Non notable musician.

Our Lady J
Non-notable singer.

Mateusz Jakubiec
Nonnotable pop singer

G-Marl Jamal
Non-notable musician.

Barney James
Non-notable English musician.

David James (American artist)
Non-notable musician.

Rod Janzen
Non-notable musician.

Jessica Jarrell
Non-notable musician.

Richard Anthony Jay
Non notable musician.

I am jen
Non-notable musician.

Mark Jenkins
Non notable musician

Miguel A. Jenkins
Non-notable musician: there's lots of little bits that might establish notability, but they don't quite do so.

Patrik Jensen
NN musician.

Shin Jimin
singers are not notable outside of his group, AOA (band).

Paul J Johnson
Appears to be a non-notable singer.

Viktor Jonas
Non-notable musician.

Justin Jay Jones
nn singer

Daniel Jorgensen
Not a notable musician, in a nutshell.

Sarah June
Non-notable musician.

DJ K1000
Non-notable musician.

KUBA Ka
Nonnotable musician.

Nastia Kamenskikh
Non-notable singer as she only has 41 hits on Google.

Rory Kaplan
Non-notable musician lacking non-trivial support.

Sijadu kaPotelwa
Minor local singer in South Africa.

Tamar Kaprelian
Non-notable singer/actress with one non-chart single, no album, one minor acting role.

Kastro (rapper)
Musician who is not notable outside of the group he's a member of.

Vena Kava
Singer in a barely notable death metal band.

My Name Is Kay
Musician of uncertain notability, who's had one very minor semi-hit single and has yet to release an actual album.

Kerfew
Non-notable musician.

Even Kern
Singer/songwriter/producer with single album.

Tom Kershaw
Non-notable teen musician.

Joe Kessler
Non notable musician.

Daniel Keys
Non-notable musician.

Khalia
Unsigned singer.

Khingz
A non notable hip hop artist.

Heart Break Kid
Non-notable musician.

DJ Kidd
No indication it meets the criteria for musicians.

Jess King
NN musician.

Jeramie Kling
Unremarkable musician, unnotable outside the band he's in.

Samuli Kosminen
Non-notable musician.

Kottarashky
Non-notable musician lacking GHit and GNEW of substance.

Slobodan M Kovačević
Non-notable musician.

Erlend Krauser
Non-notable musician.

Armen Ksajikian
Non-notable musician/actor

Jimmy Kunes
non notable musician

Kwes
Non-notable musician.

Kyle (rapper)
Artist doesn't appear notable.

Alex Lagemann
Non notable musician.

Casey Lagos
Musician of questionable notability.

Jeremy Larson
Seems like a fairly successful musician, but he is hardly Notable.

Lisa LaRue
Non notable musician.

Kim Last
Singer with questionable notability, not sure how notable the show she was on is though either.

Tom Laverty
Notability is questionable as a musician.

Richard Laviolette
Non-notable musician.

Gregory Lebaube
Musician with no indication of notability.

Damien Lecointe
Non-notable musician.

Annabel Lee
Apparently non-notable musician.

Jesse Lee
Non-notable singer with but one released single.

Leo LeVox
Non-notable musician.

Michelle Lewis
Unnotable singer.

Lifestyle (band)
Non-notable side project of an almost non-notable musician.

George Von Liger
Non-notable new musician.

James Light
Completely non-notable singer.

James Limborg
Although the artist has toured with notable artists (the Jets and Prince) there is no indication that he has notability on his own.

Philip Lindholm
Non-notable singer/actor/whatever.

John Adidam Littlejohn
Non notable Musician.

Rex Liu
Not a notable musician.

Luis Livingstone
Unremarkable musician.

Donny B. Lord
Non-notable musician lacking
GHits of substance and GNEWS.

Gordon J Lovie
Non-notable musician/songwriter.

Babar Luck
Non-notable musician.

IL Lusciato
Non notable musician

Ise lyfe
Non notable musician.

Logan Lynn
Non-notable musician.

Ann Maartmann
Non-notable singer.

Mike Maas
Seemingly non-notable musician.

MeLa Machinko
Non notable musician.

Jason Maek
Non notable singer with only 2
releases so far

Mahdar
Non-notable musician.

Wolf Mail
Non-notable musician.

Anton Maiof
Non-notable musician.

Tunit malcom
Unremarkable musician.

April Malmsteen
Wife of a notable musician.

Tony Manshino
Artist who's released a few albums
on minor labels, but doesn't seem to
meet any of the criteria for notable
musicians.

Rob Martino
non notable musician

Peter Mason
Non-notable musician.

Young Mass
Non notable musician.

Miljenko Matijevic
Singer for notable band, but is not
individually notable as a musician.

Nicholas Matthews
Non-notable musician.

Mav (rapper)
Non notable musician.

Koby Maxwell
Non-notable musician/actor lacking
Ghits and GNEWS of substance.

Edward Maya
Non-notable singer.

Bryan McAllister
Musician who may have recorded with 2 bands of questionable notability on Mediaskare Records.

Jess McAvoy
Non-notable musician that has not charted.

Fergus McCormick
Non-notable musician; only albums were self-released.

Dre Mcfly
Non-notable musician.

Molly McGinn
Non-notable musician and filmmaker.

Calley McGrane
NN musician.

Eric mckinney
Non-notable musician/music producer.

Steven McLachlan
Non-notable musician.

Brannon McLeod
Non-notable musician lacking ghits and Gnews for substance.

Thia Megia
Subject fails notability requirements for musicians.

Nishit Ashokkumar Mehta
Not an obviously notable singer.

Young Merc
Non-notable musician.

Dwain Messer
Non-notable musician; second nom.

Metis (American musician)
Non notable musician.

Mesropyan Mger
Non-notable singer.

Kill Miami
Singer who seems to fall under too soon

Baya Michaelson
The subject fails general notability and notability for musicians.

Lee Miles
Non-notable musician.

J Miller
Non Notable musician, google search turns up no hits

Cale Mills
Unremarkable musician in a band that plays for somebody else's solo career.

Circuit MOM
Non-notable drag queen and musician (as a musician, has no reviews nor has he charted).

MC Mooks
Non-notable musician.

MOON-kana-
non-notable singer.

Dustin Moore
Non-notable musician.

Charlie Morgan
Session musician who has not
become notable.

Rashad Morgan
Thoroughly nonnotable singer`'

Timothy Gene Morrison
Non-notable musician.

John Mott (rhythm guitarist)
Non-notable musician in a non-
notable band

MowJoe
Non-notable musician.

Shiladitya Mukhopadhyaya
No ounce of third party notability
other than the fact that married
to an Indian singer called Shreya
Ghoshal.

Kai mullins
Non-notable musician...

Thiago Live Music
A musician that has only released
one single.

Nate musiq
Non-notable musician.

Omer Nadeem
Seemingly non-notable musician.

Imtiaz najim
Non-notable musician.

Connie Nassios
Non-notable musician.

Nayrok
Non-notable musician with no
albums released.

Hafez Nazeri
Non-notable musician.

Nerone (rapper)
Appears to not meet notability for
musicians.

Warner Newman(Singer)
Unsigned artist.

Le-Tuyen Nguyen
Non-notable musician.

Alex Niedt
Non-notable musician.

Ryah Nikole
Does not appear to be a notable
musician.

Mark Nilan Jr.
Non-notable musician.

Lil nims
Non-notable musician.

Damon Noone
Non-notable singer and politician.

Nosajthing
Not a notable electronic music artist.

Gabi Novak
non notable person/ singer

Beit Nun
Non-notable musician.

Theo Obrastoff
Non-notable musician.

Sissel & Odd
Two solo artists making one record together does not establish a duo

Mehmet Okonsar
Non-notable musician.

Ahmed Tarek Ola-abaza
Non-notable musician.

Vanessa Oliveira
Non-notable singer, no record deal or releases to date.

Matt Oliver
Appears to be NN musician.

Audience of One
nn high school band of a current indie musician.

Know One
Non notable musician.

Dan Gregory Orchestra
Apparently non-notable musician/ band.

OSAMDEVETTRI
Non-notable musician.

Aslan Osiris
Musician who is non-notable outside of the group The Birthday Massacre (no notable solo releases—mostly free downloads, no membership in any other notable band, etc.).

Blake Overstreet
Non-notable musician.

Lee Daniel Owen
Non-notable musician.

Jan Ozveren
Non notable musician.

Yvette Paaoski
Did a google search and didn't get result on a musician.

Kestrin Pantera
Non-notable musician.

London Paris
Non notable band or singer.

Clive Parker
Non-notable musician.

Dj Patrick
Non-notable musician.

Michael Peace
Non notable singer.

Charice Pempengco
Unnotable musician.

Oliver Penn
Non-notable musician.

Gonçalo Pereira
Not notable as a musician.

Blair Perkins (Singer)
Non-notable musician.

Joe Perkins
A non-notable singer.

Nadia Petrella
Non-notable singer.

Phenom (band)
Does not meet notability criteria
for musicians and ensembles

Phạm Nguyễn Lan Phiên
Not-yet notable musician; could
have been speedied.

Phutureprimitive
Non-notable musician.

Level Pi
Musician who appears not to be
notable.

Disturbed Picture
Non-notable musician.

John Pilla
Non notable musician, notability
not inherited.

Candice Pillay
Non-notable singer/model.

Neal Pinto
Non-notable musician.

Artas Pitkauskas
Non-notable singer.

Chris Pittman
Extremely non notable musician.

PkoloTheproducer
Singer with questionable notability

Tone Poet
Non-notable musician.

A.V. Pooja
Not notable playback singer in
Hindi and Tamil movies.

Alan Pownall
Lead singer of a not notable band.

Schuyler Iona Press
Non-notable singer lacking Ghtis
and GNEWS of substance.

Anne Price
Non-notable musician

Prints (band)
nonnotable musicians

Not Profane
Non-notable musician/person.

Will Pugh
Unremarkable musician.

Jan Pulsford
Non notable musician/composer/
programmer/producer.

Pumpkin
Non notable musician.

Keith Pyle
Non-notable musician.

Matthew Quek
Unremarkable singer.

Quf
Fails criteria for musicians and
ensembles.

Shameer Aziz Quidwai
Non notable "singer" who seems
to have participated in a reality
contest based on the format of
American Idol.

Kamal Raja
Non-notable musician, doesn't meet
any relevant standards.

Bart Ramsey
A Jazz musician.

Rasmich
Singer with only one album, looks
like a too soon issue.

Abdolreza Razmjoo
Non-notable musician.

Pied Piper Records
Non-notable label and non-notable
musician

Recyclone
Non-notable musician.

Veda Beaux Reves
Non-notable drag queen and non-
notable musician.

DJ Rhettmatic
Non noatable musician.

Carl Ricco
Non-notable musician.

Ne' Richa
Non notable musician.

Solomon Richard
Non-notable musician.

Alberto Rigoni
Musician with no indication of
current notability.

Devonté Riley
Fails notability criteria for
musicians

The Kidd Rizz
An electro hop musician and dance
artist.

Andrew "Squirrel" Roberts
A musician of very dubious notability.

Phil Robinson (American musician)
Apparently non-notable musician.

Anthony Rodriguez (pianist)
Non notable Musician.

Kris Rodriguez
Musician notability in question

Billy Rogers
Musician with very little notability.

Steve Rokks
Non-notable "producer, musician, and mixer" who has " worked on various albums to-date.

Devyn Rose
Non-notable singer lacking GHits and GNEWS of substance.

Jo Rose
A singer with just one album so far.

Keith Rosier
Musician's autobigraphy.

William Red Rossi
Non-notable musician.

Kevin Roy
Apparently non-notable musician.

Rukas
Non-notable musician.

Ed Rush
Obscure self-published musician, without a notable record label.

Kidd Russell
Non-notable musician.

Pinky beecroft and the white russians
Non notable band of a moderately notable musician.

Mike Sabath
Non-notable musician.

Sabrina (American singer)
Non-notable singer with only an internet-release single.

Saga (singer)
Non-notable artist.

Sain
Non notable musician.

Remon Sakr
Non-notable musician.

L.a. salami
Non-notable musician.

J-M Salo
Non notable musician.

Early Wynn Salter
Non-notable musician.

Queen Samantha
Non-notable musician.

Carlton Samuels
Non-notable session musician.

Jacob Sartorius
nonnotable singer.

Saskrotch
Non-notable Internet musician.

William G. Scanlon
Non-notable college age musician.

Jerry Schmitt
Non-notable musician.

Lafrae Olivia Sci
Non-notable musician.

Harrison Scott (singer)
Non-notable musician.

Serio
nn musician

Tiago shade
Non-notable musician.

Shahaan Shaukat
Does not appear to be a notable musician.

Dean Shostak
Non-notable musician.

Zhang Shuwen
Non-notable musician.

Sebastian Sidi
Seemingly non-notable musician.

Silver (dance music)
Entirely non-notable artist.

V sinizter
Non-notable musician.

Skin (Japanese band)
Group composed of notable Japanese musicians, but the group itself has only performed together once four years ago, never toured, never released anything, and has done nothing since.

Jason Sloan
NN musician.

Nathan smart
Non notable singer.

Jan Smigmator
Appears to be a non-notable musician, who graduated from a music conservatory 3 years ago.

Cedric Smith
Non-notable producer/writer/ session musician.

Ray V. Smith
The subject appears to produce calendars featuring musicians.

Steve Smooth
Musician of questionable notability.

Smoothvega
Non-notable musician.

Lee So-jung
Singer with questionable notability.

Omid Soltani
Non-notable musician.

Festival of New Songs
Non-notable music festival for new
and unknown musicians.

Sozmusician
Non-notable musician.

Jeremy Spencer (drummer)
nn musician.

Moe! Staiano
NN musician.

Jana Stanfield
Non-notable musician.

Thomas John Stanford
Non-notable musician.

Marcus Stanley (pianist)
Not-very-notable musician, who
is best known for having been
attacked and shot; now uses that
incident as the basis for a career as
an inspirational speaker.

Wendy Starland
Does not appear to meet the
notability criteria for musicians and
ensembles.

Addison Steel
Seemingly not notable musician/
songwriter.

Mark Stenberg
Non-notable musician.

Jimmy Stevens
Unremarkable musician, no chart
success or critical attention of any
note.

Barry Stock
Non-notable musician.

Clay strom
NN high school aged "rap artist"
who hasn't had a single release yet.

Decomposed Subsonic
Non notable musician

Prodigal Sunn
Non-notable rap musician.

Kevin Sunray
Non-notable musician.

Karel Susanteo (Singer)
Singer that falls under too soon

Merlin Sutter
Musician with little notability to be
found.

Robert Svilpa
Nonnotable unsigned musician.

Syler
Non notable musician.

T-Shyne
Seemingly non-notable musician.

Maryam Tashaeva
Fails notability criteria for
musicians.

Skatemaster Tate
Non-notable musician.

Shloime Taussig
Non-notable singer.

Teejay (singer)
Potentially non-notable singer.

King tef
Non-notable rap artist.

Tempo
Subject does not meet notability
standards for musicians.

Juelz Terea
Simply put, a non-notable musician.

Breaking the Illusion
Non-notable musician: no album
releases, no hit singles.

Ayak Thiik
Non-notable singer/songwriter.

Mini thin
Non notable musician.

Dywane Thomas Jr.
Non-notable musician.

David R. Thompson (Singer)
Unremarkable "musician".

Uziah Thompson
Non-notable session musician.

Alan Thurlow
Musician with questionable
notability.

Phil Thurston
Musician who primarily writes for
advertisements, and hasn't really
made much of an impact.

John Tielli
Not notable solo musician that has
been a member of a number of
bands.

King Tiger (Rapper)
Non-notable musician.

Louis Tomlinson
Singer of questionable individual
notability.

Michael Tomlinson
non notable musician

ToTs (rapper)
Non-notable musician.

Jitta On The Track
Non-notable musician.

Traphik
non notable "musician"

Gradimir Trifunovic
Non-notable musician.

TristanV
Non-notable musician.

Will Tucker
Not notable 18-year-old musician.

Mike Turco
Non-notable musician.

Milo Turk
Unsigned musician known primarily for his song No Sex Allowed.

Dejuan Turrentine
Non notable musician.

Carl Tuttle
Non-notable musician lacking GHits and GNEws of substance.

Shocker tv
Non notable musician.

TxHustla
nn musician without a record contract, apparently, who releases his own mixtapes under his own label.

Kassie Tyers
Singer who does not meet the notability criteria.

Rick Uncapher
Non-notable musician.

Uwe Ungerer
Non-notable musician.

Destined Universal
Non-notable musician.

Steve Vansak
non-notable musician

Tom Vanstiphout
Unnotable musician.

Alex Vega
Non-notable musician.

Venomiss
Non-notable musician lacking non-trivial support.

Miranda Vettrus
Non-notable musician lacking GHits and GNEWS of substance.

Chris Via
Non-notable singer lacking GHits and GNEWS of substance.

Cultural Vibe
Non-notable remix musician.

Vidya Iyer
Non notable musician

Maya Vik
Non-notable musician; three paragraphs one time, even in the Dagbladet, does not constitute notability; and any obscure trash can be "sold via iTunes".

Penguin Villa
Does not appear to meet notability criteria for musicians.

Alla Vinokurova
Non notable musician.

Angel Vivaldi
Seemingly non-notable musician.

Vlad
Non-notable artist

Lejla Vulić
absolutely non-notable child singer

Shawn Wade
Non-notable musician.

Kanon Wakeshima
Unnotable singer.

Riley "Special" Wallace
Subject is a local musician in
Toronto and does not seem notable.

Brad Walst
Non-notable musician.

Wayne'M
Non-notable musician.

Rod Webber
Indie musician and filmmaker.

Little G. Weevil
A blues musician originally from
Hungary, but now lives in Atlanta
Georgia.

Gary Weight
Non-notable musician/author.

Tom Weil
NN musician/magician.

Claire Welles
Non-notable musician lacking
GHits and GNEWS of substance.

Peter Whitford (drummer)
Potentially non-notable musician.

Jody Wildgoose
Non-notable musician, does not
appear to have a critically reviewed
work or other popularity.

Steve Wilks
Non-notable musician.

Lyndi Williams
Opera singer with not much of a
notability assertion.

Winta
non-notable musician

Dan Wleklinski
Non-notable musician.

Antony Wolfson
Musician not yet notable.

Kandy Wong
Seems to be a not-yet-notable
musician who has had some film/
TV appearances.

Chuck Wright
Looks like a man with a job
(session musician) without own
notability

Fabio Wunderbar
No assertion of notability for
Austrian musician.

X Blake Freeman X
Non-notable musician.

XECFCx
Non-notable band, doesn't meet
the general notability criteria or
the criteria for musicians and
ensembles.

Kaveh Yaghmaei
Non notable musician, not covered
by third parties.

YahZarah
Non-notable singer.

Yaviah
Non-notable reggaeton "artist".

Yendri
Non-notable person (musician).

Maria Yiakoulis
Artist with no discography.

E.G. Young
Non notable musician.

Heo Youngji
The person is not notable yet as a
singer.

Eric Zaccar
A minor local playwright and
musician.

Unique Zayas
Not yet notable singer

Zdenko Ivanušić
Non-notable musician.

Asem Zhaketayeva
Non notable singer.

Robbie Zhang-Smitheram
Subject does not appear to meet the
notability criteria for musicians

Painter

Yusif Alizadeh
Unnotable painter.

Bruno Amadio
Anonymus Painter only known
for drawing The Crying Boy, a
Paranormal.

The Incredible Amoeba
Not-notable painter.

Green Andy
Nonnotable "experimental rock
artist" with a bunch of mp3 CDs for
sale

Hasmik Avetisyan
non notable painter, artist.

Rick Bartow
Just one of the hundreds of
thousands of minor painters with
a work or two hanging in a few
museums.

Carlos Botelho
Carlos Botelho (born in 1964) is
an unknown portuguese painter
who has the same name than the
real portuguese painter Carlos
Bothello (18 september 1899 - 18
august 1982). He tried to cheat the
portugueses by replacing the real
one by his autobiography, but he
failed because portugueses know the
real painter.

Jelena Dorotka
A minor painter.

Nelson Villalobo Ferrer
Non-notable painter who won
some non-notable awards.

Silvio Góes
A painter of wall like so many
others in Brazil.

Irena Kazazić
Non-notable Slovenian painter.

Josef Maršál
Possibly non-notable painter and
artist.

Vivaldo Martini
Apparently non-notable painter of
pseudo-classical portraits.

Tadeusz Matejko
Non-notable painter or works.

Shawn McNulty
Non notable abstract painter.

Janez Pristavec
Non-notable Slovenian painter.

Miranda Rumina
Non-notable Slovenian painter.

LEE Kwun-leung Vincent
Non-notable painter.

Lee Kwun Leung Vincent
Non-notable painter.

Arnaud Courlet de Vregille
Totally non-notable painter.

Genetic Zoo
non-notable artist: series of
paintings shown in one exhibition,
in the artist's own studio, fails
notability.

Photographer

Victor Avila
Non-notable photographer.

Nicholas Beatty
Non-notable photographer.

Marco Bolognesi
Non-notable photographer.

Louise Anne Brown
Non notable photographer.

The Cobrasnake
Non-notable photographer

Wilhelm Derksen
Non-notable photographer.

Max Ellis
Non-notable photographer lacking GHITS and GNEWS of substance.

Ellie Ga
Non-notable photographer.

Kim gottlieb-walker
None notable photographer.

Hasson Harris
non notable photographer

Aaron David Holloway
Non-notable photographer.

Brian Kerr
Non notable photographer.

Kike San Martín
Non notable photographer

Ronald J. Meyer
Non-notable photographer who wrote a self-published book that won an award nobody's heard of.

Thomas R. Moore
Photographer of questionable notability.

James Nisbeck
Non-notable photographer.

David Olivera
Non-notable photographer.

Iko Ouro Preto
Non-notable photographer.

Ellen Rogers
Relatively unknown photographer.

Taffi Rosen
Not notable photographer.

Den Schliker
Not a prominent fashion photographer.

Tyler Shields
Photographer with "no formal training" who has been involved in a series of events which have made the news, but not due to the quality of his photographs.

Ewen Spencer
non notable self published
photographer

Doug Tham
Non-notable photographer.

Angelo Valentino
A terribly hush-hush photographer,
a "cult pioneer" whose "compelling"
works "are often difficult to
acredit due to the fact he works
under various pseudonyms and
is, even by the standard of his
contemporary Banksy very elusive
and deliberately obscure".

Playwright

Dominic Allen (British playwright)
playwright with little performed and apparently nothing published.

Joy Basu
Playwright whose notability is not established.

Max Bush
Minor playwright.

John Carlino
Barely known playwright and politician.

Daniel McClung
Unknown NYC playwright.

Tazewell Thompson
Apparntly non-notable theater director / playwright.

Kate Toon
Non-notable playwright lacking GHits of susbstance and zero GNEWS.

James Wilkes
apparently unpublished as playwright.

Screenwriter

L. M. Kit Carson
Possibly non-notable screenwriter/
actor.

Gregory Hughes
Non notable screenwriter.

Dev Ross
Non-notable screenwriter lacking
GHIts and GNEWS of substance.

Sutapa Sikdar
Looks like a not inherited issue,
she is a screenwriter yes, but not a
notable one, her husband is more
notable it seems, maybe someday
she will get a page-but not yet.

Bobby Smith, Jr.
Non-notable screenwriter lacking
GHits and Gnews of substance.

Paul B. Stanton
Screenwriter with just one credit.

Joshua Zetumer
NN screenwriter.

Drazen Zigic
Non-notable "screenwriter" who
seems to be more famous (if
marginally so) as a blogger.

Sculptor

Julie Campagna
Unremarkable sculptor.

Albert Zambrano
Non-notable as an Architecture or
sculptor.

Unsorted

Cara A
Non-notable artist.

A.Renee
A young, non-notable artist.

Michele Abeles
Non-notable artist.

Michiyo Akaishi
Non-notable manga artist.

Cody Alain
Non notable makeup artist.

M. A. Alford
Non-notable artist.

Michael Alford
British artist of little apparent notability.

Achraf Amiri
Non-notable artists.

Boris Amstislavski
Non-notable artist.

Anakrid
Appears to be a non-notable artist.

DJ Baby Anne
Non-notable artist.

Cotman, Anni
Non-notable artist.

Arahmaiani
Non-notable artist.

Beth Armstrong
Non-notable artist.

Scotty Arsenault
Non-notable artists.

Javi du art
Non-notable artist.

Edgar Carrasco Arteaga
Non-notable artist.

Henry Hudson: Artist
Non-notable artist lacking GHits and GNEWS of substance.

Asa Asika
IMO fails notability - he is the manager of a non-notable (IMO) artist

Bruce B
Non notable artists / record label boss.

Audrey Bagley
Non-notable artist lacking non-trivial support.

Lucille D. Bainbridge
Non-notable artist.

Tova Balman
Non-notable artist lacking non-trivial support.

Bimal Banerjee
Non-notable artist.

George Bary
Non-notable artist.

Math bass
Non-notable artist.

Brandon Bauer
Non-notable artist lacking non-trivial support.

Butch Bautista
Non-notable tattoo artist.

Cat Beach
Non-notable artist with only one published album

Mark Bern
Non-notable artist who only just debuted a few years ago.

Kishore Pratim Biswas
Non-notable artist.

Julien Le Blanc
Non-notable artist.

James Blinkhorn
Non-notable artist.

Christina Di Bona
Unknown artist of dubious notability.

Jai Boo
An underground artist current working on their first solo release,
but that's just a mixtape.

Sly Boogy
Non-notable musical artist.

Fiona bowie
Non-notable artist.

Michael G. Breece
Artist lacks notability, discography has only 2 entries of dubious notability.

Bridget Irish
Seems to be a non-notable local artist.

Kadar Brock
Non-notable artist.

Ramon Bruin
Artist who had his 15 minutes of fame on the internet last year.

Adam Buenz
Local stained glass artist with no indications of notability.

Gunther Burpus
Non-notable artist.

C-tru
Non-notable artist.

Kutt Calhoun
Non-notable artist.

Renato Cataldi
Non-notable artist.

Julia lindsey chot
Non-notable artist.

Mike Compton
Apparently entirely non-notable beyond playing with a few notable artists?

Abner Cope
May not meet the notability criteria for artists.

Francisco Sanchis Cortés
Non-notable artists.

Josh Courtoreille
Relatively unknown (87 ghits) musical artist.

Rosz Craig
Non-notable artist.

Finders Keepers Crew
Apparently non-notable group of street artists in London.

Skill U.T.I Crew (Los Angeles Graffiti Artist)
Non-notable graffiti artist lacking GHits and GNEWs of substance.

Andrew Crossley
Probably non-notable comics colorist.

Tom Cullberg
Non-notable artist.

Jesse Dee
Non-notable artist.

Hail Destroyer
No artist, no nothing.

Joe DeVito
Non-notable artist.

Leslie Dick
Non-notable artist.

James Dietz
Non-notable artist.

Daz Dillon
Non-notable recording artist.

Milan Dobrojevic
non-notable fractal artist.

Trigga Da Don
Non-notable rap artist.

Károly Doncsecz
An obscure potter.

Doorly
Non-notable dubstep artist.

Mark Dougherty
non notable artist.

Veronika Drahotova
Unknown artist.

Catherine Duc
Non notable artist

Michael Duffy (Irish Artist)
Non-notable Irish artist.

Matt Duke
Subject is a recording artist on a
student-run record label.

Caggie Dunlop
Person has been a player in one
small tv show - perhaps will
become notable and become a
singer and recording artist but they
are not yet as the external supports
show.

Tony Dupe
Non-notable artist.

Andrew Dutkewych
Non-notable artist.

Jean Edelstein
Possibly a non-notable artist.

Andy Von Eich
Not a notable artist.

Kyle Jacob Ellis
fictional artist, information, person

Jill Emery
Fails notability both as an artist and
as a musician

Alex Emsley
Non-notable artist.

Dempsey Essick
Well-meaning but non-notable local
artist.

Jon Paul Fiorentino
Not notable artist.

Peter Flemming
Non-notable artist.

Fluidism
Appears only on referenced artists
website.

Clay Foster
Non-notable artist lacking non-
trivial support.

Nicholas Friesen
A non-notable artist.

Alex G
Completely non-notable YouTube
cover artist.

Goran Gatarić
Completely non-notable artist.

AKA George
Does not meet the notability
criteria for music artists.

Grisha Georgiev
Fails to meet ARTIST requirements.

Tommaso Geraci
Unremarkable artist.

Rob Gibsun
Non-notable artist.

Rexhep Goçi
Non notable artist.

Colin Goldberg
Non - notable artist.

Goldin+Senneby
non-notable artists.

Anthony Gomes
Borderline notable artist.

Steph Goodger
Little known artist in France.

Leon Goodman
Non notable artist.

Victor Gordon
Non-notable artist lacking GHITS and GNEWS of substance.

Yannis Grammaticopoulos
Non-notable artist.

Ha-Ha (street artist)
Seemingly NN street artist.

Sherman Halsey
The awards he won aren't terribly valid assertations of notability either: GAC and CMT are fan-voted; MTV is apparently awarded to the artist; and only the ACM award is of any validity.

Fain Hancock
Non notable artist, mention in the NY Times is clearly trivial at one line.

Heather Hannoura
non notable artist.

Sonia Hansman
Non notable artist.

Don Ed Hardy
Tattoo artist and self-published author.

Henry Charles Heffer
Non-notable artist.

Michael Hesp
Non notable artist.

Gina Heyer
Non-notable artist.

HiFyve
Non-notable music artist.

Eric Himan
Non-notable artist, no assertion of artist notability.

Christopher Hogan
Non notable artist.

Susana Hong
non notable make up artist.

Jodi J Horne
Non-notable artist.

Chieko Hosokawa
Non-notable manga artist.

Mark Humes
Non-notable artist/broadcaster lacking non-trivial support.

Tai Hustle
Non-notable recording artist.

Joe Jacks
Non-notable artist - zero non-wikipedia Google hits for "Silver and Spiders" OR "Silver & Spiders"; no relevant hits for "Joe Jacks"+artist or " Benjamin Jacks"+artist.

Jasif
Non-notable member of Students Federation of India and mimicry artist.

Jesuton
Not notable artist.

Christoff Johnson
Looks like a non notable artist.

Yolanda Johnson
Non-notable artist with little or no media attention, no charting songs.

JonOne
Granted, as a graffiti artist and painter, it's somewhat difficult to establish yourself, there is essentially nothing on "JonOne" that establishes him as a noteworthy individual.

Judal
Non-notable manga artist.

Mc Keezy K
Notability of the artist questionable

Natsumi Kawahara
Non-notable manga artist.

Charles Napier Kennedy
Doesn't seem to be much more than a locally-known artist from 100 years ago.

DJ Kentaro
Non notable artist.

Bahador Kharazmi
borderline artist.

Drasko Klikovac
Non-notable artist

Rydah J. Klyde
Non-notable artist on barely notable record label.

Naoshi Komi
Non-notable artist.

Scott Koziol
Bassist-for-hire who has played with some notable artists but does not appear to be notable on his own.

Eisaku Kubonouchi
Not notable as an artist/animator.

Iou Kuroda
Unnotable manga artist.

Hidenori Kusaka
Unnotable manga artist.

Angelica Leight
Non-notable new age artist.

Louis St. Lewis
Non-notable artist.

Steven Johnson Leyba
Artist performing and promoting an obscure method of painting that seems to only be notable within a small niche crowd.

Kirk Little
Artist of dubious notability.

Lodekka
Non-notable artist

Liz Looker
Non-notable artist.

Ruth Lorenzo
Non-notable artist.

Sudarsan Yennamalli M.
A young artist with only one exhibition to his credit.

Adamo Macri
An artist working on a project for which he's made a bizarre choice of "important contributors to the treasury of culture".

Jennifer Maestre
Notability not established, does not meet ARTIST.

Miltos Manetas
Non notable visual artist.

Carol Mann
Non-notable watercolour artist.

Peter Mars
Non-notable artist.

Anna May-Rychter
Non-notable artist.

Roberto Márquez
non-notable artist.

Daria McGrain
Non-notable comics artist.

Ron McKelvey
Non-notable former con artist.

Medo Ismail
Non-notable artist.

DJ Mehedi
Non-notable artist, only self-references.

Marsha Mellow
Non-notable drag artist.

Gustavo Mendonca
Seemingly non-notable video game artist.

MisterMN
Non-notable artist.

Hitomi Mizutani
Non-notable manga artist.

Modeo
Non-notable artist.

DJ Mondo
Non-notable artist.

Rajesh More
Minor fashionista who works as costume designer in Telugu film industry.

Tobias Morgan
Non notable artist.

Stéphanie Morissette
Appears to be a non notable artist.

Harry Moskowitz
MMA artist with only two top tier fights both losses.

Dave Moyer
Non-notable artist and technique.

Suman Mukherjee
Not notable mime artist.

Eva Navarro
Non-notable artist

Neo-Gothic
Non-notable group which seems to exist only to promote one artist (the twice-deleted Charles Moffat).

Dodo Newman
Does not meet the ARTIST guidance.

Jean-Frédéric Noël
Non notable artist.

TJ Norris
Non-notable artist.

Sandile Nzuza
Seems to fail notability criteria for artists.

Rev. Nørb
Non-notable artist.

Izzy O'Kay
Non notable artist.

Angela Oberer
NN voiceover artist.

Susan Olmetti
Non-notable artist.

Skot Olsen
Non-notable artist

Alvaro Orlando
Contestant is only known for "one thing", which is winning a reality show (The Pickup Artist).

Suzanne Kendall Osborne
Non-notable artist.

Simone Otis
non notable makeup artist.

Beacham Owen
A non-notable motorsports artist who had a brief motorsports career.

Jessica Owen
Non notable artist.

Gregory Allen Page
Non-notable artist

James Parman
Non notable artist.

Melvin Pather
Non-notable artist.

Tiffany Patterson (choreographer)
Non-notable choreographer.

50 Pence
Non notable artist.

Morgan delle Piane
Notability as an artist not established, nor is family enough to support significance.

Pilar Pili
non-notable artist.

Anthony Pitt
Non-notable artist.

Angelo Plessas
Not notable visual artist.

Ron e Polo
Non-notable artist.

Porno
Totally non-notable artist.

Jason Porter
Non-notable rap artist.

Frank Michael Preuss
Not notable as an artist.

Giuseppe Prinzi
Non-notable artist.

Privatelektro
Unknown group of artists with no reputation or noticeable success.

Purple Pussy
Closest thing to notability is a lawsuit from the artist.

Iza Radinsky
Non-notable artist.

Kenneth Brown Ransley
Non-notable artist.

Regilio
Non-notable artists.

Rene "brewedsosweet" Reyes
Non-notable artist.

Atarah Richmond
Non-notable artist.

Adrian Rigby
A wildflife artist whose reputation (and extreme hyperbole on his website) seems to be based on winning 3 awards at an exhibition of the Wildlife Art Society.

Shani Rigsbee
Does not appear to be a noteworthy artist.

Anita Rodriguez
Non-notable artist.

Gary Rohrabaugh
Non-notable artist.

Therese Steinhardt Rosenblatt
Non-notable artist with no documented accomplishments other than one 10-day exhibition at a non-notable gallery and a purchase by the Metropolitan Museum, which appears to have decommissioned the work.

Stacey Rozich
Non-notable artist lacking GHITS and GNEWS of substance.

Noel Rudloff
Seems to be a non-notable artist.

Alan Russell-Cowan
An artist known only as he was the main person to be featured in a film of schizophrenia.

Joop Sanders
Potentially non-notable artist.

Matthew Santoro
Non-notable visual effects artist and even less notable aspirational director of yet-to-be-made films.

Hasan Fuat Sari
Non-notable artist.

Sash!
Artist doesn't appear to be notable.

Rigel Sauri
Minor artist, notability not established.

Eric Schlittler
Non-notable recording artist.

Jakob Senneby
Non-notable artist.

Shanell (aka SnL)
non notable musical artist

Suvigya Sharma
Non notable artist.

Lee Shi-min
Non-notable artist.

Ahlam Shibli
Artist of very questionable notability.

Shipititez
Seemingly non-notable artist.

Tom Sierak
Seems to be a non-notable artist.

Dan Sites
Sites is an artist who has done album covers.

Biggy Smallz
Only info on the artist was from the usual webcrawling sites, allmusic and yahoo music.

Corey Smith
The questions of notability of an artist

Mickey Smith
Non-notable artist.

Damien Smith
Non-notable artist.

Wendy Son
Not a notable artist.

Yumi Song
non-notable artist.

Spirit Spine
Non-notable musical artist.

Kid Springs
Non-notable artist, albums and record label.

Midi the Squirrel
Non-notable furry artist.

John Stango
Non notable visual artist.

Twank Star
non notable musical artist

Eric Stephens
non-notable comic strip artist

Stereotyp
Non-notable artist.

Young Stunna
Another Nigerian upcoming artist, struggling to be notable.

Love Systems
Seemingly non-notable company that offers seminars on seduction/"pick-up artist " tactics.

Natalija Šeruga
A non-notable Slovenian artists.

Rose Tang
Not a notable artist.

Marc Tasman
Doesn't seem like a notable artist to me.

Teachr
Appears to be NN artist lacking non-trivial support.

Mohamed Temam
Non-notable artist.

Tosca Teran
Not notable - very minor artist

Diana Thater
Not notable artist.

Pavel Tichon
Non-notable media artist.

Tjaša Iris
A non-notable Slovenian artist.

Daniel Toledo
Possible non-notable artist.

Simon Toparovsky
Non-notable artist.

Fabio Torres
Non-notable artist

John Trujillo
Non-notable layout board artist (that's a pretty minor role in film post-production).

Born Twice
Non-notable early release from a notable artist.

Dorico Alonzo Tyree
Artist is non notable.

Ana Tzarev
non-notable artist, only assertion of notability is that she borrowed money to open an art gallery

Olav Harald Ulstein
Only of local interest, both as a politician and as an artist.

Danilo Ursini
Non-notable artist.

Anette Vedvik
Norwegian artist appears to be non-notable.

Gerrit Verstraete
Non-notable artist.

Sylvia Villagran
Non-notable voiceover artist.

Michael Vincent-Rori
non-notable living artist

Elena Volkova
Artist which does not appear to meet notability standards.

Shawn Vulliez
Flash artist with no real notability of his own aside from the Ultimate Showdown of Ultimate Destiny flash, no notable google hits aside from an extremely fleeting mention on wsj.com.

Waconzy
Another Nigerian upcoming artist, struggling to be notable.

Michael Weismore
Non-notable artist who apparently only currently has notability in the Syracuse, New York area.

Aaron Wexler
NN artist

Joy Whitlock
Non-notable CCM artist.

Michael W. Wooten
Non-notable artist.

Jerry Wray
Unnotable artist.

Alii wright
Non notable artist.

Xiaoze Xie
non notable artist.

Bernat Ylla
Non notable artist.

Ali Zamani
The artist's website looks like an
ad for video services; his portfolio
includes commercials, web design,
wedding photography, and some
music videos.

Sergio Zavattieri
Non-notable artist.

About this book

Every day, people on Wikipedia nominate articles for deletion and discuss whether they should remain in the encyclopedia or not. This is done on a sub page called "Articles for deletion". A frequent reason for exclusion of an entry is "non-notability".

After I had a look at those discussions, the article about my own person (Gregor Weichbrodt) ironically became nominated for deletion from the German Wikipedia, too. The anonymous person that put me on the list wrote "Completely misses notability criteria for 'authors'. Unsatisfying notability criteria for artists too."

I wrote a Python script to download the contents of every "articles for deletion"-page from the past ten years and filter the results by artistic occupation. I saw that I wasn't alone in my fate and that there were many more non-notable artists in this world who also failed to meet the notability criteria. This book is dedicated to these artists.

Gregor Weichbrodt,
September 2016

Acknowledgments

With thanks to Kathrin Passig and Hannes Bajohr for discussions on the matter, and Christiane Frohmann for pointing out the Wikipedia pages and suggesting a poetic project. Further thanks go to to Karl Flender, Vicki Bennett, Ranjit Bhatnagar, Carl Bamber and Julia Pelta Feldman.